JOB SEARCH
BASICS

THIRD EDITION

by
Michael Farr

MOST
CORRUPT

JIST Works
America's Career Publisher

Job Search Basics, Third Edition

© 2006 by JIST Publishing, Inc.

Published by JIST Works, an imprint of JIST Publishing, Inc.
8902 Otis Avenue
Indianapolis, IN 46216-1033

Phone: 1-800-648-JIST   Fax: 1-800-JIST-FAX
E-mail: info@jist.com   Web site: www.jist.com

Quantity discounts are available for JIST products. Have future editions of JIST books automatically delivered to you on publication through our convenient standing order program. Please call our Sales Department at 1-800-648-5478 for a free catalog and more information.

Acquisitions Editor: Barb Terry
Development Editor: Joyce Nielsen
Production Editor: Jill Mazurczyk
Cover Designer: designLab
Interior Designer: Marie Kristine Parial-Leonardo
Interior Layout: Marie Kristine Parial-Leonardo
Proofreaders: Linda Seifert, Jeanne Clark
Indexer: Tina Trettin

Printed in the United States of America
11 10 09 08 07 06   9 8 7 6 5 4 3 2 1

We have been careful to provide accurate information in this book, but it is possible that errors and omissions have been introduced. Please consider this in making any career plans or other important decisions. Trust your own judgment above all else and in all things.

Trademarks: All brand names and product names used in this book are trade names, service marks, trademarks, or registered trademarks of their respective owners.

ISBN-13: 978-1-59357-313-3

ISBN-10: 1-59357-313-8

About This Book

This workbook will help you find a job. First, you will read about ideas that are important in the job search process. Then you will interact with these ideas through questions and worksheets. Be sure to keep a pen or pencil handy! When you search for a job, remember what you learned here and look back through your answers as needed.

The following special features appear in this book:

 Example. Examples usually feature a conversation between two people about someone's struggles and successes in the job search process. Learn what works—and what doesn't—with these real-world discussions.

 Think About It. It's time to stop reading when you see the light bulb. Take a few minutes to think about what you just read. Answer the questions in the best way you can. Don't rush! When you are done writing, continue reading the book.

 Checkpoint. Checkpoints appear at the end each chapter and help you review what you have just learned.

 Challenge. After each Checkpoint is a Challenge where you can apply your knowledge.

 Focus. These thoughts appear in the graphic you see at the left. For extra guidance and inspiration, don't miss these boxes.

 Worksheets. Worksheets are identified by this image. All worksheets contain clear directions to help you practice and interact with the concepts in the book.

Table of Contents

PART 1: IDENTIFY YOUR SKILLS FOR SCHOOL, WORK, AND LIFE 1

CHAPTER 1: TAKE CONTROL OF YOUR LIFE 3
Are You Doing What Is Important to You? 3
This Is Your Life 3
What Does It Mean to Take Responsibility? 4
Accepting Responsibility Is Good for You 5
Your Time: Do You Spend It Well? 7

CHAPTER 2: WHAT ARE SKILLS? 14
Defining Skills.................................14
Breaking Apart Your Skills 14
Why Do You Need to Know Your Skills? 16
Knowing Your Skills Helps You Choose Activities 17
The Skills Triangle.................................18

CHAPTER 3: IDENTIFY YOUR ADAPTIVE AND TRANSFERABLE SKILLS 22
Your Adaptive and Transferable Skills 22
Your Adaptive Skills 23
Your Transferable Skills.................................26

CHAPTER 4: CREATE A SKILLS INVENTORY 34
Your Life Experience Can Help You Know Your Skills and Plan Your Career 34
Your Skills Inventory 35
Your Top Skills.................................41

CHAPTER 5: PLAN ON HOW TO BEST USE YOUR SKILLS 45
Making Your Inventory Work for You 45
Jobs That Match Your Skills 46
Gathering Information 48
If You Need More Training or Skills 49
Make a Plan.................................53
Measure Your Progress 56
Conclusion: Skills for Life.................................58

PART 2: TWO BEST WAYS TO FIND A JOB 59

CHAPTER 6: UNDERSTAND THE JOB MARKET 61
Welcome to the Job Market 61
Small Organizations Have Big Advantages...62
Where People Work 62
Traditional Job Search Sources 63
How Job Seekers Find Jobs: The "Hidden" Job Market 67

CHAPTER 7: GET READY FOR YOUR JOB SEARCH 71
Before You Start Your Search 71
Prepare an Effective Resume..75
Develop a Portfolio 77
Introducing the JIST Card® 79

CHAPTER 8: ONE OF THE TWO BEST JOB SEARCH METHODS—GETTING LEADS FROM PEOPLE YOU KNOW 84
Warm Contacts: The Most Effective Job Search Method........................84
Develop a Network of People You Know 85
Who Is in a Network?..86

CHAPTER 9: THE NETWORK IN ACTION 90
Build Your Job Search Network 90
A Network Can Work for You...95
How to Get Referrals from Your Network 96
Three Questions to Ask When Getting Referrals 97

CHAPTER 10: ANOTHER OF THE BEST JOB SEARCH METHODS—DIRECT CONTACT WITH EMPLOYERS 99
Moving from "Warm" to "Cold" 99
Find Employers Who Need You 100
The Yellow Pages—A Large Listing of Potential Employers....................100
Getting Even More Leads 103

CHAPTER 11: TELEPHONE AND EMPLOYER CONTACT SKILLS.............................105
Getting Your Foot in the Door 105
Getting to the Person Who Supervises..106
Getting an Interview..106
Tips for Making Telephone Contacts 109
Keep Calling Until You Get Through..109
Drop In on Employers 112
Conclusion: Find a Better Job in Less Time 113

PART 3: INTRODUCTION TO JOB APPLICATIONS 115

CHAPTER 12: APPLICATION BASICS 117
What Is an Application Form? 117
Why Employers Use Applications 117
Make a Good Impression 122
Preparation: The Key to Successful Applications 129
System-Prompted Applications...129

CHAPTER 13: GATHER INFORMATION FOR YOUR APPLICATION...............132
Gathering the Facts...132
The Power of Words 132
Deal with Negative Information 134
Your Application Inventory 135
What Is a Reference?..157

CHAPTER 14: HOW TO USE AN APPLICATION IN YOUR JOB SEARCH...............167
Put It All Together..167
Answers to the Applications Review Quiz 168
Making Applications Work for You 169
Gary's Completed Application 172
How Gary Got the Interview 172

CHAPTER 15: PRACTICE WITH APPLICATIONS..176
Putting Pen to Paper..176
Conclusion: Create a Good Impression with Your Application 186

PART 4: WHY SHOULD I HIRE YOU? 187

CHAPTER 16: WHAT IS AN INTERVIEW? 189
Don't Wait for the Job to Open!...189
Interviewing Now May Save an Employer Time and Money 191
Good-Worker Traits..191
Know Your Job Objective 192

CHAPTER 17: WHAT AN EMPLOYER EXPECTS 195
Employers Want Solid Evidence...195
Three Clues That Employers Look for in Interviews 195

CHAPTER 18: THREE-STEP PROCESS FOR ANSWERING INTERVIEW QUESTIONS—GIVING THE RIGHT CLUES...202
Handling Interview Questions 202
Good Listening Helps You Give Good Answers................................204
Practicing the Three-Step Process for Answering Interview Questions 204
The Question of Pay 216
What If You Can't Answer an Interview Question?...........................217

CHAPTER 19: BUILD CONFIDENCE FOR YOUR INTERVIEWS 220
An Interview Is No Time to Be Modest 220
Talk About Your Best Points and Speak with Self-Confidence 220
You Can Ask Questions in the Interview, Too 223
Closing the Interview 224
After the Interview—Follow Up! 225

CHAPTER 20: GET READY FOR THE INTERVIEW AND YOUR NEW JOB 230
Are You Ready? 230
Surviving on a New Job 231
Conclusion: Stay Confident 241

INDEX 242

part 1

Identify Your Skills for School, Work, and Life

- Chapter 1: Take Control of Your Life
- Chapter 2: What Are Skills?
- Chapter 3: Identify Your Adaptive and Transferable Skills
- Chapter 4: Create a Skills Inventory
- Chapter 5: Plan on How to Best Use Your Skills

You already have hundreds of skills. For example, you can read this sentence, something that no other animal can do. Today you got up and got to wherever you are now, on your own, something that no machine or computer can do by itself.

You can think, make decisions, interact with people, follow instructions, solve problems, move objects, and do all sorts of things that science cannot yet duplicate. When you really think about it, the skills you have are amazing.

Part 1 of this book was written to help you understand the many skills you have or want to develop. It will also help you *use* these skills to make good decisions in your education, career, and life.

chapter 1

Take Control of Your Life

THE GOALS OF THIS CHAPTER ARE

- To understand what it means to accept responsibility
- To discover why taking responsibility helps you live a more satisfying life
- To analyze how you spend your time

ARE YOU DOING WHAT IS IMPORTANT TO YOU?

In Part 1 of this book, you will learn how to identify your key skills. These are your skills that you like to use and are good at. You will learn how to use these and other skills to help you succeed in school, in work, and in life.

FOCUS

The choices you make determine the quality of your life.

But before you learn more about your skills, you should first think about what is most important in your life. You should also think about how you want to spend your time. That is what this chapter is about. Later, you can decide how to apply your key skills to activities where you want to spend your time.

THIS IS YOUR LIFE

Ask yourself these questions:

1. Whose life are you living?

2. Whose life should you be living?

3. Whose life do you want to be living?

Life is full of questions. The questions present choices. It's up to you to make the choices that work best for you.

No one knows you better than you know yourself. No one ever will. When it comes to your life, *you* are the expert.

Now answer these questions:

1. How can I create the best life possible for myself?

2. Do I feel I'm totally in control of my life?

Consider these questions carefully. Give them a lot of thought. They are some of the most important questions you will ever have to answer.

 think about it

On the following lines, write down some ideas about what you think it means to be totally in control of your life.

_____

_____

_____

_____

_____

WHAT DOES IT MEAN TO TAKE RESPONSIBILITY?

Taking responsibility means that you

- Don't blame anyone else for what happens to you
- Don't try to control anyone else
- Do take credit for what you do right
- Do admit that you make mistakes
- Do promise to learn from every mistake

- Do consider the results of your actions before you act.

Learning to take responsibility for yourself is very hard. Everyone has problems with this at one time or another. Many people never learn to be completely responsible.

It is hard to be responsible, but it is worth the effort. In the following chapters, you'll see that accepting responsibility is a "key" skill—one that helps you get along in life.

ACCEPTING RESPONSIBILITY IS GOOD FOR YOU

When you accept responsibility for your life, you gain power. You are no longer under anyone else's control. Your thoughts are your own. Your feelings are your own. You own yourself.

When you blame other people for what happens to you or for how you feel, you lose power. You give it away. You're saying to those people, "You have more power over how I feel than I do. You have more power over what I think, and what happens to me, than I do."

What this means is that those people have control over you. Do you want other people to control your life? Or do you want to take control for yourself?

Accepting responsibility gives you the power to be in control of your own life. It frees you to make choices. It lets you take the opportunity to get what you need and want in your life—even if that means taking risks.

You might feel afraid of making choices and taking risks. Everyone does. But it's part of taking control. And taking control is one of the keys to living a truly satisfying life.

EXAMPLE

Learning to Take Responsibility

Susan and John are friends. They go to the same school, and they take many of the same classes. They even started working at a local flower shop at the same time.

(continued)

(continued)

EXAMPLE

Susan enjoyed working at the flower shop, but John did not. John didn't like taking orders, and he had trouble arriving at work on time. Eventually, John quit the job to look for an easier job.

Meanwhile, Susan enjoyed working at the shop, but she was having trouble with her job responsibilities. Her math skills were poor, and her supervisor was disappointed with the mistakes she was making with inventory and the cash register. Her supervisor told her that even though she had a good attitude, she would have to leave the job if she kept making mistakes.

Susan: So, John, how's the job hunt going?

John: Not very well. I almost had a job at the sporting goods store, but the boss wanted me to work both days on the weekends!

Susan: I really like my job at the flower shop, but I've been having some trouble with the math that it takes to do the work.

John: That's not your fault. Boy, those people really work you too hard!

Susan: They don't work me too hard. They just want me to make good business decisions and give the customers the correct change. After all, making too many mistakes could really hurt the profits. I would like to run my own business some day, and I wouldn't want someone working for me who makes math mistakes again and again.

John: Running your own business? Girl, that sounds like a real hassle! So how are you going to keep your job at the flower shop?

Susan: I enrolled in two night classes—one for business studies and the other for math.

John: You're taking business and math classes? Not me! I already took math. My math teacher was really bad. It's probably his fault I can't find a job!

Susan: When I took math before, I really wasn't concentrating very well. Some of it was hard, so I concentrated on other subjects. This time, at night school, it's going to be different.

Susan realized that only she could make a difference in developing her skills and being a good employee. She had made some mistakes in the past, but she took responsibility for them and corrected them.

John blamed others for his "bad luck." When something went wrong, he figured that there was no way he could change his situation.

Soon, Susan started making improvements in her job. The manager was impressed that she was learning additional business and math skills on her own. Susan worked very hard in her classes and eventually got a promotion.

John continued looking for a job without much luck. Every time he faced an opportunity, he found a reason to avoid it. He always had an excuse.

 ## think about it

On the following lines, list the areas in your life where you want more control. It can be anything from finding the time to study more, to learning a new job skill, to eating the right foods.

_____

_____

_____

_____

_____

Now review your list. Are you are willing to accept total responsibility for each of these areas? Place a check mark beside the ones that you are.

YOUR TIME: DO YOU SPEND IT WELL?

Are you stealing from yourself? Time is like money. If you use it all up on things that aren't very important, you are cheating yourself. You don't gain anything of value.

You may own lots of things, but they don't mean much if you don't have the time to enjoy them. Or you may waste so much time that you don't do the things that are really important to you.

Time is precious. Wasting your time is like stealing your most valuable possession.

Time-Tracking Worksheet

During the next seven days, keep a record of how you spend your time. Use the "Time-Tracking Worksheet" on the next pages to see how you actually spend your time.

In the "Activity" column, write down each activity you do that day. For example, "Ate breakfast," "Went shopping," "Went to work," "Watched TV," "Talked on the phone."

In the "Time" column, write down when you started the activity and when you stopped, as in "6:30–6:45 a.m.," "9:00–11:00 a.m.," and so on.

In the "Benefits to Me or Others" column, write how this activity helped or hurt you or someone else. It might have had good effects like "Helps me relax" or "Enjoyed time with a friend" or "Jogging keeps me in shape."

You may find that some activities do not help you. They may keep you from doing something more important, like studying or spending time with friends.

For example, spending three hours at night playing a computer game may "Keep me from reading." These notes will help you identify activities you want to change.

Activity	Time	Benefits to Me or Others
Monday		
_____	_____	_____
_____	_____	_____
_____	_____	_____
_____	_____	_____
_____	_____	_____
_____	_____	_____
Tuesday		
_____	_____	_____
_____	_____	_____
_____	_____	_____

_____   _____   _____

_____   _____   _____

_____   _____   _____

_____   _____   _____

Wednesday

_____   _____   _____

_____   _____   _____

_____   _____   _____

_____   _____   _____

_____   _____   _____

Thursday

_____   _____   _____

_____   _____   _____

_____   _____   _____

_____   _____   _____

_____   _____   _____

Friday

_____   _____   _____

_____   _____   _____

(continued)

(continued)

_____	_____	_____
_____	_____	_____
_____	_____	_____
_____	_____	_____
_____	_____	_____

Saturday

_____	_____	_____
_____	_____	_____
_____	_____	_____
_____	_____	_____
_____	_____	_____
_____	_____	_____

Sunday

_____	_____	_____
_____	_____	_____
_____	_____	_____
_____	_____	_____
_____	_____	_____

 **think about it**

After you tracked your time for a week, what did you learn about yourself? How do you spend most of your time? The worksheet that follows asks you to add up your time spent doing the same activity throughout the week.

In the left column on the next page, list the five activities in which you spent most of your time. In the right column, list the five activities you enjoyed doing the most. Compare the columns.

How I Spent the Most Time

1. _____
2. _____
3. _____
4. _____
5. _____

What I Enjoyed Doing Most

1. _____
2. _____
3. _____
4. _____
5. _____

Are you spending enough time on the things that are important to you? How could you spend more time on the things that matter the most to you? Write your notes on what you learned.

_____

_____

_____

_____

_____

_____

checkpoint

After completing this chapter, answer these questions. They will help you review what you learned. Your answers will also help you decide how you can use what you just learned.

1. How can you take control of your life?

_____

_____

_____

2. Why is it good for you to take responsibility for yourself?

_____

_____

_____

3. How do taking responsibility for yourself and the way you use your time relate to each other?

_____

_____

_____

4. How can you spend more time doing what you want to do and what you like to do?

_____

_____

_____

challenge: Develop Awareness of Responsibility and Time

Think of someone you know who complains often about "how life is treating" him or her. Then write answers to the questions below. (This exercise is not meant to criticize someone. But you can learn from looking at the behavior of others.)

1. Does this person seem happy? Why or why not?

   _____

   _____

   _____

2. Does this person blame other people for his or her situation in life? If so, what do you think of this?

   _____

   _____

   _____

3. Does this person take responsibility for his or her life? If so, how? If not, what makes you think this way?

   _____

   _____

   _____

chapter 2

What Are Skills?

THE GOALS OF THIS CHAPTER ARE

- To understand what skills are
- To see why knowing your skills can help you in your learning, career, and life
- To learn about the kinds of skills that are most important to you

DEFINING SKILLS

A skill is something you can do. Reading, writing, and cooking a meal are examples of skills. A skill can also be part of your personality. You might be skillful at getting along with others or good at organizing things.

Most activities require sets of skills that can be broken down into smaller skills. If you can learn to do the smaller skills, the whole activity becomes much easier to master.

BREAKING APART YOUR SKILLS

Driving a car is just one example of using many sets of skills in order to do an activity. Here are just some of the skills needed to drive a car:

- Reading road signs
- Eye-hand coordination
- Parallel parking
- Applying the brakes and accelerating correctly in different situations

- Understanding road maps and directions
- Concentrating
- Backing up
- Avoiding dangerous situations
- Knowing how to operate all controls
- Interpreting information from rearview mirrors

As you can see, it takes many skills to drive a car. You may not realize how many skills you already have. Most people have hundreds of skills. You probably do, too. Does that surprise you? Like most people, you have probably developed some skills much more than others.

 ## think about it

Think about all the skills you use now. They can be skills you use in school, at work, at home, or elsewhere. Write them in the spaces below. You can list the same skill in more than one column.

School Skills	Work Skills	Leisure Skills
_____	_____	_____
_____	_____	_____
_____	_____	_____
_____	_____	_____
_____	_____	_____
_____	_____	_____
_____	_____	_____
_____	_____	_____

Which of these skills are you best at using? Place a check mark next to the skills you think you are best at. Which ones do you most like to use? Place a double check mark next to these skills.

The skills with the most check marks would be your best skills. However, you have many, many more skills, even if you haven't fully developed them yet.

WHY DO YOU NEED TO KNOW YOUR SKILLS?

The things that you are good at and the things that you enjoy doing are an important part of who you are. Throughout our lives—in school, in work, and in our free or leisure time—our skills become a central part of our lives.

That is why you enjoy some school classes more than others. Whatever work we choose, we are happiest when we do work that is satisfying and meaningful to us.

> ## FOCUS
>
> *Your best skills are the ones you do well and enjoy using.*

It may be unpaid work such as raising children, part-time work, or work that we have been trained and educated to do.

The same is true for how we spend our leisure time—we are happier when we spend time in ways that are satisfying and meaningful to us.

 think about it

Think about your favorite classes and what you most enjoy doing at work and in your leisure time. Answer these questions:

1. What classes have you enjoyed the most?

   _____

   _____

2. What work do you enjoy doing so much that you would do it for free?

   _____

   _____

3. What things do you most like to do in your leisure time?

   _____

   _____

KNOWING YOUR SKILLS HELPS YOU CHOOSE ACTIVITIES

Listed below are several reasons why you need to know your skills:

- So you can choose activities that you enjoy and will best meet your needs.
- So you can best plan for your additional learning or leisure needs.
- So you can use your best skills to get a satisfying job.

Let's look at these reasons in more detail.

Choosing Activities That You Enjoy and Will Best Meet Your Needs

If you know what you are good at and enjoy doing, you are much more likely to do those activities. You won't waste time doing things that aren't important to you. Satisfaction in your life activities is directly related to using skills that you enjoy. So it makes sense to know what those skills are.

Planning for Your Learning or Leisure Needs

If you are clear about what you enjoy, you can decide to learn more about a hobby, sport, or other activity you want to do. You could do the following:

- Read magazines or use the Internet to learn more.
- Join a club or team related to your interest.
- Talk to someone who enjoys this activity.
- Simply schedule more time in this activity.

Using Your Best Skills to Get a Satisfying Job

Knowing your skills is very important in deciding the type of job you want.

Whenever you go to a job interview, the most important question that you'll have to answer is "Why should I hire you?" Any employer is going to expect you to be able to answer that question.

You can't just say, "Because I'm a nice person" or "Because I really need to make some money." You'll have to convince an employer that you have the skills to do the job.

> ## FOCUS
>
> *You have a better chance of being hired if you can communicate your skills to an employer.*

Many job applicants don't know how to do that. They don't know how to talk about their skills or their good worker traits.

Even though you have hundreds of skills, some will be more important to an employer than others. And some will be far more important to you as you decide what sort of job you want.

In the next section, you will learn about three major types of skills. This will help you prepare to use your best skills in planning your education, your career, your leisure time, and your life.

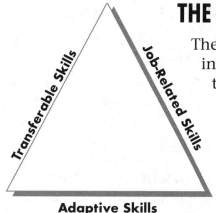

THE SKILLS TRIANGLE

The "Skills Triangle" is a system that groups your skills into three major types. Most people don't think of the things they can do as skills. The Skills Triangle will help you remember the types of skills you have. Later, knowing that you have a variety of skills will help you understand yourself—and better plan your education, your career, and your life. Let's now learn more about each part of the Skills Triangle.

Adaptive Skills or Personality Traits

These are skills you use every day to survive and get along. They might be skills you have learned, or they could be part of your basic personality. Adaptive skills are also called self-management skills. They help you get along in different situations.

Some examples of adaptive skills are the following:

- Honesty
- Enthusiastic attitude
- Ability to follow instructions

Transferable Skills

These are general skills that can "transfer" from job to job. For example, good communication skills are useful in many different jobs. Transferable skills are very important to employers.

Some examples of transferable skills are as follows:

- Being able to manage people
- Solving problems
- Keeping track of money

Job-Related Skills

These are skills a person must know to do a specific job or type of job. The job can't be done without these skills. For example:

- An auto mechanic must know how to tune engines and repair brakes.

- A teacher must be able to present information in a way that students can understand.

- An administrative assistant must be able to use a computer and communicate well.

Job-related skills are important, but they are not the most important thing that an employer considers. Often an employer will be willing to train an employee to learn the necessary job-related skills. The employee must have the right adaptive and transferable skills to get the job, but the job-related skills can sometimes be learned on the job.

The "Think About It" that follows shows why transferable and adaptive skills can get you hired for a job, even if you don't have all the job-related skills right now.

 think about it

Imagine that you are the manager of a local delivery company. You have one job opening and two job applicants to choose from. You are looking over your notes about each applicant. Here are your notes:

Applicant 1: Has experience as a delivery truck driver. Checked with previous employer. Was late for work fairly often. Missed some deliveries. Good driving record. Couldn't find location of delivery on several occasions, and left customers without supplies. Doesn't seem real motivated.

Applicant 2: No experience on this type of job. Previous employer says applicant hardly ever missed a day of work, was always on time, and dependable. Very enthusiastic. Seems eager to learn.

Which applicant would you hire? In the space that follows, explain why.

_____

_____

_____

_____

_____

Chances are, an employer will choose the same person for the same reasons you did. In the next chapter, you'll work with worksheets to identify your best skills of the three types in the Skills Triangle.

 ## checkpoint

After completing this chapter, answer these questions. They will help you review what you just learned.

1. What are skills? Give some examples of your skills.

   _____

   _____

   _____

2. How can knowing your skills help you find the job you want?

   _____

   _____

   _____

3. Explain what the three types of skills are and tell which ones are most important to an employer.

   _____

   _____

   _____

4. How can knowing your skills actually save you time?

   _____

   _____

   _____

challenge: Develop Your Skills Awareness

Think of a job that might interest you. Find out everything you can about the skills that are involved in doing that job. You can do this by talking to someone you know who does this job. You can go to the library and ask for a book on career information. You can search for the job on the Internet and connect to related sites.

Several books we recommend are the *Occupational Outlook Handbook, Young Person's Occupational Outlook Handbook, America's Top 300 Jobs, Exploring Careers*, and the *New Guide for Occupational Exploration*. Internet sites that provide job descriptions and other career information include one run by the government at www.bls.gov and another run by JIST at www.careeroink.com. After you have gathered information about the skills needed, answer these questions:

1. What job-related skills do you already have for this job?

   _____

   _____

   _____

2. What job-related skills would you have to learn?

   _____

   _____

   _____

3. What transferable skills do you already have for this job?

   _____

   _____

   _____

4. What adaptive skills do you already have for this job?

   _____

   _____

   _____

chapter 3

Identify Your Adaptive and Transferable Skills

THE GOALS OF THIS CHAPTER ARE

- To identify your skills

- To understand how you can use your skills in learning, career, leisure, and life planning

- To begin learning how to communicate those skills

YOUR ADAPTIVE AND TRANSFERABLE SKILLS

In Chapter 2, you learned about three types of skills. They are as follows:

- Adaptive skills/personality traits
- Transferable skills
- Job-related skills

When you identify your best skills in each of these groups, you can do the following:

- Make good decisions about your learning, career, and leisure options.

- Answer the most important question an employer will ask: "Why should I hire you?"

YOUR ADAPTIVE SKILLS

On the following lines, list three things about yourself that help you get along in life or that make you a "good" person. Take your time.

1. _____

_____

_____

2. _____

_____

_____

3. _____

_____

_____

These three traits may be some of the most important things you need to know about yourself. They define the way you see yourself and what you have to offer others.

Many people think these skills or traits are not important enough to talk about, but they are. In a job interview, for example, mentioning these traits may get you hired over someone who actually has more experience than you do.

 ## Adaptive Skills Worksheet

This worksheet contains a list of adaptive skills. The first group of skills—"Basic Adaptive Skills"—is the most important one. Many employers will not hire an applicant who does not have these skills. The second group of skills is important for many jobs.

Look over the list and put a check mark beside any skill that you feel you have now. In the "Want to Improve" column, put a check mark beside any skill that you feel you need to improve. (Later we will go over ways to develop and improve your skills.)

At the end of the worksheet, you can add other skills that you feel you have now or want to improve that are not listed here.

(continued)

(continued)

Basic Adaptive Skills

Skill	Have Now	Want to Improve
Good attendance	❑	❑
Honest	❑	❑
Arriving on time	❑	❑
Following instructions	❑	❑
Meeting deadlines	❑	❑
Hard working	❑	❑
Getting along with others	❑	❑

Other Adaptive Skills

Skill	Have Now	Want to Improve
Ambition	❑	❑
Patience	❑	❑
Flexibility	❑	❑
Maturity	❑	❑
Assertiveness	❑	❑
Dependability	❑	❑
Learn quickly	❑	❑
Complete assignments	❑	❑
Sincerity	❑	❑
Motivation	❑	❑
Problem solving	❑	❑
Friendliness	❑	❑
Sense of humor	❑	❑
Leadership	❑	❑
Physical stamina	❑	❑
Enthusiasm	❑	❑
Good sense of direction	❑	❑
Persistence	❑	❑

Skill	Have Now	Want to Improve
Self-motivated	❑	❑
Accept responsibility	❑	❑
Results oriented	❑	❑
Willing to ask questions	❑	❑
Pride in doing a good job	❑	❑
Willing to learn	❑	❑
Creative	❑	❑

More Adaptive Skills (Add your own.)

Skill	Have Now	Want to Improve
_____	❑	❑
_____	❑	❑
_____	❑	❑
_____	❑	❑
_____	❑	❑
_____	❑	❑
_____	❑	❑
_____	❑	❑

Your Top Adaptive Skills

Review your list of adaptive skills. Then, in the spaces below, list the three adaptive skills that you feel are most important for an employer to know about you.

1. _____

2. _____

3. _____

Adaptive Skills to Improve

Now list the three adaptive skills that you feel are the most important ones for you to work on improving. (Keep these in mind for later. We'll work on improving skills in a later chapter.)

1. _____

2. _____

3. _____

<table>
<tr><td>

REMEMBER

- Adaptive skills are more like "who you are."

- Transferable skills are "things you do."

- Some skills can go into either group.

</td></tr>
</table>

YOUR TRANSFERABLE SKILLS

Adaptive skills are more like "personality traits" or "who you are," while transferable skills, like being organized, are "things you do." Many skills, like "accept responsibility," could be put into either group. Don't worry about this in making your lists. There is some overlap, and it just isn't that important to worry about.

On the lines below, list three of your transferable skills. Remember, these are the skills that you can take with you from job to job. It is important for you to know these skills so you can share them with a potential employer.

1. _____

2. _____

3. _____

There are hundreds of transferable skills. The worksheet that follows includes the ones that are most important to employers. Are the skills you listed included on the worksheet?

 ## Transferable Skills Worksheet

The skills on this worksheet are organized into clusters. This is to help you identify major types of jobs that will suit you best.

Read the list and put a check mark beside each skill that you feel you are strong in. Then go through the list again and put another check mark in the "Use in Next Job" column if you think you want to use that skill in your next job.

Note: Jobs that tend to pay more or have more responsibility often require one or more of the "key" skills at the beginning of the worksheet. If you have any of these skills, you will want to emphasize them to potential employers.

Key Transferable Skills (These are very important to employers.)

Skill	Already Strong	Use in Next Job
Meeting deadlines	❑	❑
Planning	❑	❑
Public speaking	❑	❑
Budgeting and money management	❑	❑
Supervising others	❑	❑
Instructing others	❑	❑
Accepting responsibility	❑	❑
Managing people	❑	❑
Meeting the public	❑	❑
Working effectively in a group	❑	❑
Organizing projects	❑	❑
Taking risks	❑	❑
Self-controlling	❑	❑
Self-motivating	❑	❑
Detail oriented	❑	❑
Knowledge of basic computer skills	❑	❑
Can explain things to others	❑	❑
Problem solving	❑	❑
Good writing skills	❑	❑
Good math skills	❑	❑

Other Transferable Skills: Working with Things

Skill	Already Strong	Use in Next Job
Using my hands	❑	❑
Assembling things	❑	❑

(continued)

(continued)

Skill	Already Strong	Use in Next Job
Building things	❏	❏
Constructing, repairing buildings	❏	❏
Making things	❏	❏
Observing, inspecting things	❏	❏
Driving or operating vehicles	❏	❏
Operating tools and machinery	❏	❏
Using complex equipment	❏	❏

Other Transferable Skills: Working with Data

Skill	Already Strong	Use in Next Job
Analyzing data, facts	❏	❏
Auditing records	❏	❏
Investigating	❏	❏
Using the Internet	❏	❏
Sending and receiving e-mail	❏	❏
Researching and locating information	❏	❏
Calculating, computing	❏	❏
Classifying data	❏	❏
Counting	❏	❏
Observing	❏	❏

Other Transferable Skills: Working with People

Skill	Already Strong	Use in Next Job
Patient	❏	❏
Sensitive	❏	❏
Social	❏	❏
Tactful	❏	❏
Teaching	❏	❏
Interviewing others	❏	❏

Skill	Already Strong	Use in Next Job
Listening	❑	❑
Tolerant	❑	❑
Understanding	❑	❑
Kind	❑	❑
Diplomatic	❑	❑
Counseling people	❑	❑
Confronting (when necessary)	❑	❑
Trusting	❑	❑
Can be firm	❑	❑

Other Transferable Skills: Using Words and Ideas

Skill	Already Strong	Use in Next Job
Can be logical	❑	❑
Speaking in public	❑	❑
Designing	❑	❑
Editing	❑	❑
Remembering information	❑	❑
Writing clearly	❑	❑
Corresponding with others	❑	❑
Creative	❑	❑

Other Transferable Skills: Using Leadership Ability

Skill	Already Strong	Use in Next Job
Arranging social functions	❑	❑
Competitive	❑	❑
Motivating people	❑	❑
Can be decisive	❑	❑
Running meetings	❑	❑

(continued)

(continued)

Skill	Already Strong	Use in Next Job
Delegating	❏	❏
Working out agreements	❏	❏
Planning	❏	❏

Other Transferable Skills: Using Creative, Artistic Ability

Skill	Already Strong	Use in Next Job
Dancing, body movement	❏	❏
Drawing, art	❏	❏
Performing, acting	❏	❏
Playing instruments	❏	❏
Presenting artistic ideas	❏	❏
Music appreciation	❏	❏
Expressive	❏	❏

Other Transferable Skills: Add Your Own

Skill	Already Strong	Use in Next Job
_____	❏	❏
_____	❏	❏
_____	❏	❏
_____	❏	❏
_____	❏	❏
_____	❏	❏
_____	❏	❏

Your Top Transferable Skills

Review your worksheet of transferable skills. List below the five that you are best in or that are most important to you.

1. _____

2. _____

3. _____

4. _____

5. _____

Transferable Skills to Improve

Now list the five skills you most want to improve. (We'll work on improving your skills later.)

1. _____

2. _____

3. _____

4. _____

5. _____

In the next chapter, you will create an "inventory" of your experiences. This listing of experiences can be used to help you uncover even more skills, including job-related skills.

 checkpoint _____

After completing this chapter, answer these questions. They will help you review what you just learned.

1. What are adaptive skills?

_____

_____

_____

2. What are transferable skills?

_____

_____

_____

3. Why is it so important for you to know and be able to communicate your adaptive and transferable skills?

_____

_____

_____

challenge: Practice Communicating Your Skills

Look back at the three top adaptive skills that you listed. Think about situations in your life when you used each of those skills. Briefly describe those situations and how you used the skills. Can you support your claim that you have these skills? (This becomes very important during job interviews.)

Adaptive Skill 1

_____

_____

How I used this skill:

_____

_____

_____

_____

_____

Adaptive Skill 2

_____

_____

How I used this skill:

_____

_____

_____

_____

_____

Adaptive Skill 3

_____

_____

How I used this skill:

_____

_____

_____

_____

_____

chapter 4 _____

Create a Skills Inventory

THE GOALS OF THIS CHAPTER ARE

- To create a skills inventory using your life history
- To use your skills inventory to support your key skills
- To use your skills inventory to identify job-related skills
- To use your skills inventory to plan education, career, or leisure activities

YOUR LIFE EXPERIENCE CAN HELP YOU KNOW YOUR SKILLS AND PLAN YOUR CAREER

In Chapter 3, you used worksheets to identify your adaptive and transferable skills. These were two of the types of skills from the Skills Triangle.

In this chapter, you will be gathering information about yourself from all the experiences that you have had. In these experiences are keys to two important considerations:

- Who you are
- What you have spent time and effort on

These are also keys to what you do well now and what you are likely to do well in the future.

YOUR SKILLS INVENTORY

Completing the worksheets that follow will help you form a skills inventory. With this inventory, you will see that many of your life experiences can support your adaptive and transferable skills. The inventory can also help identify your job-related skills, the third group of skills from the Skills Triangle.

Job-related skills don't just come from jobs you have had or have been trained for. You probably have many skills that you have developed through a variety of activities.

The skills inventory you put together in this chapter will be very important to your career and life planning.

This knowledge can be used to help you make good decisions about your career, more education, or how you spend your leisure time. And it can help you get a good job. For example, you have a better chance of convincing an employer to hire you when you can prove your skills.

Your skills inventory will help you do the following:

- Identify more skills.
- Identify your interests and accomplishments.
- Describe experiences that explain and support your skills.

Skills Inventory Worksheet

Complete the worksheet that follows to target the key experiences and skills you gained through education, work, volunteer activities, and other experiences.

The worksheet asks you to list in the left column things you studied or did, and in the right column, skills you strengthened or gained as a result. For example, one young man listed his literature class on the left. On the right, he noted:

"Big help to me in learning to think and write. I even learned to analyze situations and how other people solved problems. My reading and communications skills got better, too."

Education and Training

Junior High School

On the following lines, include junior high school coursework that relates to your job interests.

(continued)

(continued)

Subjects Studied	Skills Strengthened or Gained
_____	_____
_____	_____
_____	_____
_____	_____

On the lines below, include any special organizations that you participated in, whether in or out of junior high school. These might be clubs, teams, hobby groups, and so on.

Extracurricular Activities	Skills Strengthened or Gained
_____	_____
_____	_____
_____	_____
_____	_____

High School

On the lines below, include high school coursework that relates to your job interests.

Subjects Studied	Skills Strengthened or Gained
_____	_____
_____	_____
_____	_____
_____	_____

On the lines below, include any special organizations that you participated in, whether in or out of high school. These might be clubs, teams, hobby groups, and similar groups.

Extracurricular Activities   **Skills Strengthened or Gained**

_____   _____

_____   _____

_____   _____

_____   _____

_____   _____

After High School

In this section, list any education or training you had after high school. Include training you have received in the military, if any.

Subjects Studied   **Skills Strengthened or Gained**

_____   _____

_____   _____

_____   _____

_____   _____

In this section, list activities and organizations that you participated in after high school.

Activities   **Skills Strengthened or Gained**

_____   _____

_____   _____

_____   _____

_____   _____

(continued)

(continued)

Work History

For this section, you will list all the jobs you've had and what your responsibilities were. In the right column, list the skills you strengthened or gained. Include part-time jobs, summer jobs, or self-employment such as mowing lawns or babysitting.

Job and Responsibilities   **Skills Strengthened or Gained**

_____   _____

_____   _____

_____   _____

_____   _____

Job and Responsibilities   **Skills Strengthened or Gained**

_____   _____

_____   _____

_____   _____

_____   _____

Job and Responsibilities   **Skills Strengthened or Gained**

_____   _____

_____   _____

_____   _____

_____   _____

Job and Responsibilities   **Skills Strengthened or Gained**

_____   _____

_____   _____

_____   _____

_____   _____

Volunteer Experience

You don't have to have been paid for work to have valuable work experience. In this section, list any volunteer work you have done, and the skills you strengthened or gained while doing it.

Volunteer Job and Responsibilities	Skills Strengthened or Gained
_____	_____
_____	_____
_____	_____
_____	_____

Volunteer Job and Responsibilities	Skills Strengthened or Gained
_____	_____
_____	_____
_____	_____

Volunteer Job and Responsibilities	Skills Strengthened or Gained
_____	_____
_____	_____
_____	_____

Volunteer Job and Responsibilities	Skills Strengthened or Gained
_____	_____
_____	_____
_____	_____

(continued)

(continued)

Hobbies, Leisure Activities, and Other Life Experiences

For this section, list hobbies, special interests, family activities, or any other activities that have led you to develop specific skills. Take plenty of time to think and remember. You have many more skills than you realize!

For example, maybe you help take care of the younger children in your family. Doing this would help you gain skills in child care, patience, taking responsibility, food preparation, and other areas.

If you like to use your computer at home, you may have gained skills in using the Internet to find information, keyboarding and word processing, or Web page design.

Special Activity   **Skills Strengthened or Gained**

_____   _____

_____   _____

_____   _____

Special Activity   **Skills Strengthened or Gained**

_____   _____

_____   _____

_____   _____

Special Activity   **Skills Strengthened or Gained**

_____   _____

_____   _____

_____   _____

Special Activity	Skills Strengthened or Gained
_____	_____
_____	_____
_____	_____
_____	

YOUR TOP SKILLS

Now you will need to go back over the entire worksheet you just completed. Use each section to complete the lists that follow here.

Things I do best:

1. _____

2. _____

3. _____

4. _____

5. _____

Skills I most enjoy using:

1. _____

2. _____

3. _____

4. _____

5. _____

Skills I most want to improve:

1. _____

2. _____

3. _____

4. _____

5. _____

Skills I want to use in my next job:

1. _____

2. _____

3. _____

4. _____

5. _____

Congratulations! You now have an inventory to help you make valuable decisions about your life and your work.

Don't worry about figuring out your entire life goals right now. People grow and change throughout their lives, and you are bound to change, too. You can't predict the future. So make the decisions that make sense now. That's the best anyone can do.

✔ checkpoint

After completing this chapter, answer these questions. They will help you review what you just learned.

1. Were you surprised by how many skills you have acquired from your experiences? What surprised you the most?

_____

_____

_____

_____

_____

2. How can you best use your skills inventory to get a job?

_____

_____

_____

_____

_____

3. Think of a job you might want to apply for. If you were an employer, would you hire yourself for this job? What skills do you need to work on to give yourself the best chance of getting the job?

_____

_____

_____

_____

 # CHALLENGE: Think About Career Options

Have you ever dreamed of being your own boss? This could be a real option for you. Look over your skills inventory and think about the activities you enjoy the most. You might be able to combine your skills and interests to start a business of your own.

Hobbies such as gardening can turn into a landscaping business, for example. If you like woodworking, you could do furniture repair and refinishing. If you know a lot about computers, you could have a computer repair or consulting business. Some of the skills required to be self-employed are the following:

- Time management

- Marketing your service or product

- Self-discipline and motivation

- Money management

- Willing to work hard
- Locating necessary supplies or equipment
- Serving customers

Can you think of some others? Write them here:

_____

_____

_____

_____

_____

Self-employment is just one of many ways you can put your skills to work doing what you like to do. Becoming self-employed is not easy and may require a lot of preparation and work.

If you think you are interested in self-employment, many good resource books and other information are available in the library and on the Internet. If you are interested, we suggest you learn as much as you can about self-employment or starting a business.

chapter 5

Plan on How to Best Use Your Skills

THE GOALS OF THIS CHAPTER ARE

- To learn how to gather information about jobs that match your skills
- To find out ways to develop more skills
- To consider options for additional education or training

MAKING YOUR INVENTORY WORK FOR YOU

In the last chapter you spent considerable time creating an inventory of your skills and experiences. In this chapter you will learn how to use this inventory to determine which careers would be best suited to your skills. You will also learn to identify resources for further education or training.

My Best Skills

Go back through Chapters 3 and 4 to review the skills you identified as your best skills. These are the skills that you do well and may want to use in your next job. Write them again on the next page.

Transferable	Adaptive	Job-Related
_____	_____	_____
_____	_____	_____
_____	_____	_____
_____	_____	_____

Your job search will go more easily if you know your skills and can say clearly what they are. You need to be able to answer the question, "Why should I hire you?" For example, when Mike talks to people about his job search, here is what he might say to them:

> I am a hard worker and am willing to work weekends and holidays as well as during the week. I am also good with details and can follow instructions without being told what to do more than once.

> I would like to work with my hands and with people but am willing to consider other types of jobs.

My Skills Statement

On the lines below, write a statement describing your best skills. Pretend that someone has just asked you what sorts of things you can do on a job. Make the statement short and emphasize your best skills. Practice your skills statement until you sound like someone *you* would want to hire.

_____

_____

_____

_____

_____

_____

JOBS THAT MATCH YOUR SKILLS

There are thousands of job titles. Yet your task is to select just a few jobs that best fit your skills and interests. One way to do this is to consider groups of similar jobs.

The list below provides groups of jobs organized into 16 major interest areas. Later, you can go to a library and look up the jobs in the areas. For now, just check the interest areas of jobs that sound most interesting to you.

❏ **Agriculture and Natural Resources:** An interest in working with plants, animals, forests, or mineral resources for agriculture, horticulture, conservation, extraction, and other purposes.

❏ **Architecture and Construction:** An interest in designing, assembling, and maintaining components of buildings and other structures.

❏ **Arts and Communication:** An interest in creatively expressing feelings or ideas, in communicating news or information, or in performing.

❏ **Business and Administration:** An interest in making a business organization or function run smoothly.

❏ **Education and Training:** An interest in helping people learn.

❏ **Finance and Insurance:** An interest in helping businesses and people be assured of a financially secure future.

❏ **Government and Public Administration:** An interest in helping a government agency serve the needs of the public.

❏ **Health Science:** An interest in helping people and animals be healthy.

❏ **Hospitality, Tourism, and Recreation:** An interest in catering to the personal wishes and needs of others so that they may enjoy a clean environment, good food and drink, comfortable lodging away from home, and recreation.

❏ **Human Service:** An interest in improving people's social, mental, emotional, or spiritual well-being.

❏ **Information Technology:** An interest in designing, developing, managing, and supporting information systems.

❏ **Law and Public Safety:** An interest in upholding people's rights or in protecting people and property by using authority, inspecting, or investigating.

❏ **Manufacturing:** An interest in processing materials into intermediate or final products or maintaining and repairing products by using machines or hand tools.

❏ **Retail and Wholesale Sales and Service:** An interest in bringing others to a particular point of view by personal persuasion and by sales and promotional techniques.

❏ **Scientific Research, Engineering, and Mathematics:** An interest in discovering, collecting, and analyzing information about the natural world, life sciences, and human behavior.

❑ **Transportation, Distribution, and Logistics:** An interest in operations that move people or materials.

GATHERING INFORMATION

You will probably need more information to identify the jobs that interest you. You need to know about required skills and needed training or education. There may be jobs that match your skills and interests that you haven't thought of yet.

Here are some ways to find out more about the jobs that interest you.

1. Go to your school or public library and look up information in the following publications. (You can ask the librarian to help you find these and other resources.)

   ■ *Occupational Outlook Handbook:* Published by the U.S. Department of Labor, this book provides good descriptions of the top few hundred jobs in this country. It includes information on the nature of work, average pay rates, education and training required, projections for growth, and many other details.

   ■ *Young Person's Occupational Outlook Handbook:* Covers all the jobs in the *Occupational Outlook Handbook* in an easy-to-understand format.

   ■ *Top 300 Careers,* formerly entitled *America's Top 300 Jobs:* This book combines job information and job search advice. It is based on the jobs listed in the *Occupational Outlook Handbook.*

   ■ *Exploring Careers:* Written for young people, this book describes jobs in major interest areas (also called clusters), featuring people who actually work in the jobs in some of the descriptions.

   ■ The *New Guide for Occupational Exploration:* Provides details on the 16 interest areas and the many jobs available within them.

2. Talk to people who already have jobs in your field of interest. Contact employers and make an appointment or ask questions over the telephone about what skills and training you would need in order for them to hire you. Talk to a guidance counselor at a high school, vocational or technical school, or college or university about the type of jobs you are interested in.

3. If you have access to the Internet, a lot of career information is available there. The *Occupational Outlook Handbook* lists some Internet sites, and you can also get career information and links to other sites by visiting JIST's site at www.jist.com.

IF YOU NEED MORE TRAINING OR SKILLS

What if you lack some of the skills or requirements for the job you want? Let's consider what your options are.

Formal Schooling

One option for gaining new skills or improving your skills is, of course, to go to school. There are many types of schools, such as vocational high schools, colleges, universities, postsecondary vocational, technical, business, and other schools. If you are thinking about entering a school program, here are some things to consider:

- *What type of school will provide the training you need?* Some options are as follows:
  - High school career training programs
  - Community and junior colleges
  - Four-year colleges and universities
  - Vocational and technical schools

- *What is the reputation of the school?* Some things to check out:
  - Does the school have good credentials?
  - Do employers hire the school's graduates?

- *How will you pay for it?* Some options might include the following:
  - Financial aid through the school or a government program
  - Help from relatives or your employer
  - Earning enough money by working while you go through the program
  - Earning a scholarship

- *How can you arrange your schedule to make time for school?* You might have to do the following:
  - Change jobs or change your work schedule.
  - Arrange for more child care if you have children.
  - Learn to manage your time better (get up earlier or go to bed later).

- *What sacrifices are you willing to make for school?* Be prepared to do the following:

  - Give up some leisure time activities.

  - Give up things you might like to spend money on so that you can pay for school.

  - Set aside time for studying and homework.

  - Change your lifestyle.

- *What is the location of the school that best suits your needs?* You should be able to do the following:

  - Get to class meetings regularly.

  - Move if necessary.

On-the-Job Training

Some jobs do not require any formal training before you take the job. You learn by doing. This kind of job training can last from a few days to several years.

Your employer might place you under the supervision of another worker or send you to classes to train for the job.

You might also work toward a job you want in a business or organization by starting in an entry-level job. An entry-level job is often low skilled and low paying, but you can learn about the job you want to move up to. You can learn much about the organization and receive promotions if you do your work well.

Apprenticeships

An apprentice learns a trade by combining on-the-job training with classroom instruction. The program can last from one to six years.

Most programs are put on by employers, government programs, and labor unions. Bricklayers, auto mechanics, carpenters, and electricians are trade workers who learn their skills through an apprentice program.

The Military

Another option for receiving training is the armed forces. You can enlist in the service and learn job skills that you can use for a civilian job when you have finished your tour of duty.

You can also qualify for scholarships and other forms of financial aid for career training programs and even university degrees.

Local recruitment offices can help you find information about career possibilities through the military. There are books such as *Military Careers* that are put out by the U.S. government. You can also get information on the Internet at www.todaysmilitary.com.

These books contain information about available programs. Ask your librarian to help you locate this information.

Self-Directed Training

You can improve many skills by learning on your own. This is especially true of adaptive and transferable skills. Go back to Chapter 3 and look over your checklists for these skills. On the lines that follow, write down again the skills that you want to improve.

_____

_____

_____

_____

Choose the one that seems the most important right now. You should consider what will help you the most on the job you want when making your decision. Circle this skill or put a check mark next to it.

Use Your Outer Resources

There are many sources of help to improve the skill you have chosen. You could do the following things:

- Ask for help from a friend or relative who is good at that skill. ("Uncle Joe, you've always been so organized. How do you do it?")

- Find out about community programs in your area. High schools, hospitals, libraries, state universities, and many other organizations offer a wide range of adult programs on evenings and weekends. The cost is usually low.

  These programs cover both personal and practical skills. A few examples are as follows:

  - Learning math skills

  - Improving reading skills

- Learning to use a computer
- Learning how to be assertive

● Visit the library. A larger library will have many resources on education and training options and other career topics. Ask your librarian for help in finding what you need.

● Use the Internet. There are some great sites on the Internet to help young people plan their education, training, career, and life. You can find links to good sites via the major Internet service providers such as America Online or MSN. Or you can use a search engine like Yahoo.com or Google.com to find other sites on topics that interest you.

 think about it

What are some other outer resources you might use?

_____

_____

_____

_____

Use Your Inner Resources

What inner resource is most important in developing your skills? Your attitude! If you believe you will succeed, your chances of doing so increase.

The opposite is also true. If you believe you won't succeed, you probably won't. Commit yourself to a positive attitude about your goals.

STAY POSITIVE!
● Put negative thoughts out of your mind every time they come in.
● This may take a lot of practice, but if you stick with it, it will become a habit.
● Commit yourself to a positive attitude about your goals.

think about it

What are some other inner resources that you can draw on to improve your skills?

_____

_____

_____

MAKE A PLAN

You have a better chance of reaching any goal you set if you do the following:

- Make the goal very specific.
- Decide on a plan to achieve the goal.
- Gather any information you need.
- Keep track of your progress.
- Find someone to be supportive and give you encouragement along the way.
- Stick with the plan and do it!

Did you know that Thomas Edison had to try hundreds of times before he designed a light bulb that actually worked? That's a lot of "failures"! But his basic design made electricity popular and revolutionized our world. Success is often built on a series of failures.

In considering your education and career options, knowing what you _do not_ want to do is just as important as what you _do_ want to do. Planning isn't really about "failure" at all. It's about setting goals and finding ways to meet them. Edison did not fail hundreds of times, he continued to learn.

Goal Planning Worksheet

This worksheet can help you make a plan to work on a skill you've decided to improve. In this worksheet, set a SMART goal and build a plan to make it happen. A smart goal is one that is **s**pecific, **m**easurable, **a**chievable, **r**ealistic, and has a **t**ime limit. For example, the goal "I will increase my word-processing speed to 60 words per minute by June of this year" is SMART.

(continued)

(continued)

My Goal: _____

My Plan

Information I Will Gather	Do It By	Date Completed
_____	_____	_____
_____	_____	_____
_____	_____	_____
_____	_____	_____

People I Need to Talk To	Do It By	Date Completed
_____	_____	_____
_____	_____	_____
_____	_____	_____
_____	_____	_____

What I Need to Do/ How I Will Do It	Do It By	Date Completed
_____	_____	_____
_____	_____	_____
_____	_____	_____
_____	_____	_____

My Schedule

Day	Skill to Study/Practice	Time
Monday		
_____	_____	_____
_____	_____	_____
_____	_____	_____
Tuesday		
_____	_____	_____
_____	_____	_____
_____	_____	_____
Wednesday		
_____	_____	_____
_____	_____	_____
_____	_____	_____
Thursday		
_____	_____	_____
_____	_____	_____
_____	_____	_____
Friday		
_____	_____	_____
_____	_____	_____
_____	_____	_____

(continued)

(continued)

Saturday

_____   _____   _____

_____   _____   _____

_____   _____   _____

Sunday

_____   _____   _____

_____   _____   _____

_____   _____   _____

MEASURE YOUR PROGRESS

When you were a child, how did you know you were growing? Maybe someone marked your height on the wall, and each time the mark was higher than the last time. Or maybe you noticed that you could reach the faucet in the sink without using a stool.

It helps to see real results. Keeping track of your progress keeps you motivated.

Some ways to keep track of your progress are as follows:

- Buy a calendar to use only for your progress record keeping.
- Keep a journal.
- Use index cards and keep them organized.
- Use a computer program designed for tracking and record keeping. You'll be practicing a valuable skill while you're logging your own progress.
- Use a tape recorder as a spoken journal. Start each new entry with the date, and tell what you accomplished, how you did it, and how you feel about it. Talk about obstacles and how you will or how you did handle them.

 checkpoint

After completing this chapter, answer these questions. They will help you review what you just learned.

1. What are some ways to get information about jobs?

   _____

   _____

   _____

   _____

   _____

2. Are failures good or bad? Why?

   _____

   _____

   _____

   _____

   _____

3. What can you learn from risking failure?

   _____

   _____

   _____

   _____

   _____

4. How does tracking your progress help you improve your skills?

   _____

   _____

   _____

   _____

   _____

c h a l l e n g e : Focus on Goals and Strategies

Try to imagine your life ten years from now. What kind of person do you want to be? Where do you want to be living? How would you like friends, family, and co-workers to describe you? Write your answers in the spaces here.

_____

_____

_____

_____

_____

_____

_____

_____

_____

_____

_____

CONCLUSION: SKILLS FOR LIFE

Congratulations! By completing Part 1 of this book, you have taken the first step in taking control of your life. You will also be taking responsibility for everything that happens—and doesn't happen—to you.

Knowing what you can do, what you want to do, and how to do it are a big part of being successful in whatever you do. Identifying your skills can help with the first step—the rest is up to you. Make the most of your skills, and your dreams can come true.

Two Best Ways to Find a Job

- Chapter 6: Understand the Job Market
- Chapter 7: Get Ready for Your Job Search
- Chapter 8: One of the Two Best Job Search Methods—Getting Leads from People You Know
- Chapter 9: The Network in Action
- Chapter 10: Another of the Best Job Search Methods—Direct Contact with Employers
- Chapter 11: Telephone and Employer Contact Skills

Most people don't enjoy looking for a job. But you can take steps to make your job search easier. Some job search methods work better than others. We studied the research done on job search techniques. Our goal was to find the methods that did two things:

- Reduce the time it takes to find a job.
- Help you find a *better* job than you might have otherwise.

Part 2 emphasizes job search methods that can reduce the time it takes to find a job and that also tend to help you find better jobs than other methods. The two best methods are as follows:

- Getting job leads from people you know
- Making direct contacts with employers

These methods, along with other job search methods, will be covered in this part of the book.

chapter 6

Understand the Job Market

THE GOALS OF THIS CHAPTER ARE

- To learn where the best jobs are
- To learn about traditional job search methods and why they aren't the most effective
- To discover the "hidden" job market

WELCOME TO THE JOB MARKET

When you look for a job, you become part of the *job market*. When an employer looks for a worker to fill a job, that employer becomes part of the job market, too.

You need a job. An employer needs workers. The job market is where your needs meet. It is not an actual place, but it is very real.

The job market is not well organized. In fact, there really isn't any one place you can go to find out about job leads. In that sense it isn't like a market at all.

Finding a job can be confusing. For most people, it takes many weeks to find a job. But you can do certain things to reduce the time it takes. This book will show you how. It will also help you find the better jobs.

Many people look for jobs in the wrong places. It is important to know where your best chances are.

SMALL ORGANIZATIONS HAVE BIG ADVANTAGES

You hear a lot about big companies. They make the newspapers and the TV news. They are worth millions, or even billions, of dollars. They have thousands of people working for them. Big companies must be where the jobs are, right? *Wrong!*

Most nongovernment jobs are in small companies. Small companies are often overlooked by job seekers. Yet more than two out of three people work in small organizations. Small companies are also the source for over 70 percent of all new jobs.

Many large companies have laid off millions of people in the past. New and even experienced workers may find it hard to get jobs in large companies.

Small companies are also where some of the best jobs are. You can often get these jobs more easily. As you gain experience, you can often advance more rapidly.

The graphic below shows that most people work in small organizations with fewer than 250 employees.

The job search methods you learn here will help you find jobs in smaller organizations. They will also help you find jobs in government and larger organizations.

WHERE PEOPLE WORK

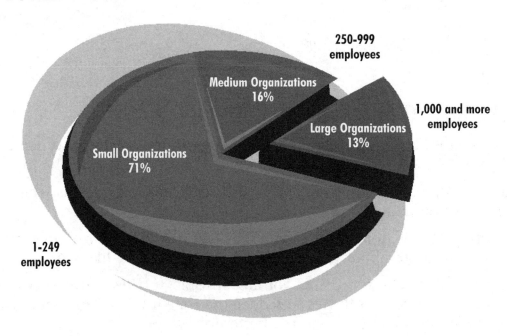

250-999 employees

Medium Organizations 16%

1,000 and more employees

Large Organizations 13%

Small Organizations 71%

1-249 employees

think about it

Think about what you just read about the job market and where people work. Answer these questions.

1. What is the "job market"?

   _____

   _____

   _____

   _____

   _____

2. Where are you likely to find the best jobs?

   _____

   _____

   _____

   _____

   _____

3. What are two reasons that small companies are a good place to find jobs?

   _____

   _____

   _____

   _____

   _____

TRADITIONAL JOB SEARCH SOURCES

You need to know where to look for jobs. You also need to know *how* to look. There are many ways to find job openings.

> ## FOCUS
>
> *Want ads and employment agencies are not the best ways to find a job.*

In this section, we look at two sources of job leads that almost all job seekers use. Just remember that these are not the only sources for job leads. These are also not the best sources. These two sources are as follows:

- Help wanted ads
- Employment agencies

Reading want ads and using employment agencies are traditional job search methods. More effective job search methods will be presented in Chapter 8. But first, let's review these more traditional job search approaches because you still may wish to use them at times.

Help Wanted Ads

Have you ever reviewed the want ads in the newspaper? A want ad might look like the item shown here:

> **Warehouse worker:** Must have good work history. Inventory control experience helpful. Some heavy lifting is required. Full time including some weekends and evenings. Fair pay and benefits. Call Ms. Henry, 722-7608 weekdays.

In a want ad, an employer advertises for a worker to fill a job opening. Many people think that looking in the want ads is one of the best ways to find a job. It makes sense, right? *Wrong!*

For every 100 job openings, only about 15 are advertised in the want ads. The other 85 are not. Believe it or not, most jobs are not advertised. And most job seekers read the want ads. That means that lots of people are applying for the few jobs that are advertised.

The Internet also lists many job openings, and we will cover this in more detail later. But, like the want ads, only a small percentage of all openings are listed on the Internet.

Does that mean that you should not read the want ads or use the Internet? No. The want ads and Internet job listings are worth reading, but you need to use other job search methods, too.

Employment Agencies

Employment agencies are another source of job leads. There are two kinds of employment agencies. The government runs one kind. The other kind is run by private businesses.

Government Employment Service

The government employment service does not charge a fee. Some unemployed people can get unemployment pay from this office. For that reason, it is sometimes called the "unemployment office."

Employers can list their job openings at the employment service. If you qualify for the job, the employment service staff will send you to interview for those jobs.

Many employers do not list their jobs here. And only about 5 percent of all job seekers find their jobs from this source. This does not sound like much, but you should still visit your local office on a regular basis.

In some areas, as many as 30 percent of the job seekers find jobs here. Some offices provide job search workshops, career counseling, and other helpful services.

The government employment service now lists most of its job openings on the Internet. If you have Internet access, you can find job postings for any region in the country at www.ajb.dni.us.

Private Employment Agencies

These agencies are businesses that charge a fee for their services. Sometimes an employer will pay the fee, but you may have to pay 15 percent or more of your first year's pay. Many agencies place want ads in the newspapers for jobs they know about. Very often, these jobs are gone by the time you answer the ad.

Only about 5 percent of all job seekers get their jobs using private agencies. Most private agencies call employers to find out about job openings. You can learn to do this yourself.

Many people do use private agencies and are happy with their services. If you do decide to use them, here are some tips:

- Ask about their fees before you go to any interviews. Ask only for job leads where the employer is paying the fee.

- Do not sign anything until you are sure you understand what you are signing. If you are pressured to sign something, ask to take the papers home to read them carefully.

- Do not agree to pay for job leads that you find yourself. Many times you can find the same job openings yourself and save the fees.

- Make sure that you continue to look for jobs on your own, even if the agency says it will get you interviews.

- Consider accepting a temporary job if this makes sense to you. Many agencies can refer you to these jobs, and many temporary jobs lead to job offers for a permanent position.

 think about it

Think about the traditional job search methods that are available to all job seekers. Answer these questions.

1. What are some traditional job search methods? (Name some you have learned here, as well as some that were not mentioned.)

_____

_____

_____

_____

_____

2. Why should you use other job search methods besides just the want ads?

_____

_____

_____

_____

_____

3. How are private employment agencies different from government employment agencies?

_____

_____

_____

_____

_____

4. How can government employment agencies help you?

_____

_____

_____

_____

_____

5. What are some reasons to use or not use private employment agencies?

_____

_____

_____

_____

_____

HOW JOB SEEKERS FIND JOBS: THE "HIDDEN" JOB MARKET

Sometimes you can find good jobs in the want ads and on the Internet. And employment agencies know about some jobs, too. But most job openings are never advertised at all. These unadvertised jobs are hidden from most job seekers.

Such jobs are part of the "hidden" job market. Most employers like to use the hidden job market. Read on to see why.

Why Employers Like the Hidden Job Market

Employers don't really like to advertise job openings. It costs money to advertise. Employers like to save money if they can.

They like to save time, too. When they place a want ad, 100 or more people might answer. The employer needs to hire only one. The employer must read all the applications or resumes and then set up interviews. All this takes a lot of time.

Saving time and saving money are two important reasons to avoid advertising. But there is another reason that is even more important.

Job seekers who answer want ads are usually strangers. Employers—who are people just like you—feel better hiring people they know something about. They don't like to hire strangers.

The next section explains how employers use the hidden job market to find workers they think they can depend on.

How Employers Use the Hidden Job Market

How does an employer find a worker to fill a job without placing an ad? Consider Frank. Frank is the manager of a grocery store called Whitman's Grocery.

Frank needs to hire someone to move and unpack boxes. He needs someone who is strong, in good condition, and can work without a lot of supervision. Most of all, Frank needs someone he can trust.

Frank does not want to have to interview a lot of people. So, he asks his other employees if they know anyone who has the skills needed for the job. Frank also talks to his friends and acquaintances. Frank hopes that someone he knows will recommend a good worker to him.

This is how employers use the hidden job market. They depend on recommendations. The hidden job market saves employers money and time. And it often helps them avoid hiring the wrong person. This book will help you learn how to find jobs in the hidden job market.

FOCUS

Traditional search methods will not help you find hidden jobs.

In this chapter, we reviewed two traditional job search methods that almost everyone uses: want ads and employment agencies. Neither way is one of the best ways to find a job. Neither way helps you tap the hidden job market.

think about it

Think about what you have learned about the hidden job market. Answer these questions.

1. What is the "hidden" job market?

_____

_____

_____

_____

2. Why do employers like to use the hidden job market?

_____

_____

_____

_____

✔ checkpoint

After completing this chapter, answer these questions. They will help you review what you just learned.

1. Do you think your best chances for finding a job are with a small or large company? Why?

_____

_____

_____

_____

2. Will you spend a lot of time responding to want ads? Why or why not?

_____

_____

_____

_____

3. Did you realize that many jobs are "hidden"? Do you have any ideas on how you might find hidden jobs?

_____

_____

_____

_____

challenge: Build Your Job-Seeking Skills

Gathering information is a valuable skill in your job search. Use the following activity to find out more about how people find jobs and what methods work best.

Talk to people you know (at least 10, if possible) about how they found their present or past jobs. Ask them to give you details.

For example, if someone used a government employment service, ask what this person did, how long it took to find a job, what the counselor was like, and other details. If someone used a private employment agency, find out what the fees were and if the person was satisfied. Find out what percentage of the people you talked with found their current job from a want ad. Write your findings in the space here.

_____

_____

_____

_____

_____

chapter 7

Get Ready for Your Job Search

THE GOALS OF THIS CHAPTER ARE

- To identify the jobs you want
- To help you prepare an effective resume and learn about portfolios
- To learn how to use a JIST Card® in your job search

BEFORE YOU START YOUR SEARCH

As you begin your job search, it's not enough to simply tell people, "I'm looking for a job." You must be clear about what type of job you want.

This chapter will help you prepare for your job search. When you do that, your job search will be more efficient and effective.

Know What Kind of Job You Want

Think about the type of job you want. The clearer you can be about this, the better people can help you. If you want to work in a clothing store, look for that type of job first. If you are looking for a part-time job, be focused on the hours you desire but flexible about the types of work you are willing to do.

Perhaps you would be willing to work in a grocery store. Maybe you would not like to work in a restaurant. The more you can tell people about what you are looking for, the more they can help you.

Job Possibilities Worksheet

In the column on the left, list jobs that interest you. In the right column, list any jobs that would definitely not interest you.

**Work That I
Would Like to Do**

**Work That I
Would Not Like to Do**

_____   _____

_____   _____

_____   _____

_____   _____

_____   _____

_____   _____

_____   _____

Now look over your list of jobs that you would like. Ask yourself, "How much do I really know about this kind of job?" Put a check mark next to any job you listed that you need more information about. Then start looking for that information.

Finding Out About Jobs That Interest You

One way to find out about jobs is to talk to people who do them. Another way is to go to your local or school library. The librarian can help you find information on careers. These resources (described in Chapter 5) are particularly helpful for most people: *Occupational Outlook Handbook, Young Person's Occupational Outlook Handbook, Top 300 Careers, Exploring Careers,* and the *New Guide for Occupational Exploration.*

Many schools, employment programs, and libraries have computer software that gives career information. Some libraries have videos on different careers. Finally, you can use the Internet for career research.

Using the Internet in Your Research

The Internet, which includes the World Wide Web (or just the "Web"), is a good source of information on just about any subject, including careers. If you haven't used the Internet, don't be afraid of it! It's much easier than you might think.

America's Career InfoNet (at www.acinet.org) is sponsored by the U.S. government and is a good place to start. You can also go to www.jist.com to get links to other career sites. America Online and MSN, two of the largest Internet service providers, offer many career resources. In addition, you can search for jobs using large job search engines such as Monster.com and CareerBuilder.com.

The more you know about the job, the industry, and the employer you are researching, the more likely you are to present yourself well in an interview. Here are some helpful Web sites for company and industry research:

- 555-1212.com, Inc. is a leading provider of online telephone and Web directory services.

- Hoover's Online (www.hoovers.com) provides information on over 14,000 public and private companies worldwide.

- InfoUSA.com is a useful site for small business owners, entrepreneurs, and sales and marketing professionals.

- Vault.com is a leading resource for career information. The Company Research section features over 3,000 company profiles from the world's top employers.

- dowjones.com, from the publishers of the *Wall Street Journal,* provides business, industry, national, and international headline news.

If you don't have your own computer with Internet access, here are some things you might try:

- Check with friends or relatives. See if someone can let you use a computer for online research.

- See if you can use school computers that access the Internet.

- Many public libraries have computer stations hooked up to the Internet. The public can use them, usually at no charge.

- Many copy stores, Internet cafes, and some coffee shops have computers with Internet access available for a fee.

If you are new to the Internet, you will need someone to help you use it. Many libraries have Internet access, and a librarian may be able to help you. If you are using someone else's computer, ask that person to help you search for career information.

A library or bookstore will probably have one or more books that will tell you how to use the Internet. Some books explain how to use the Internet to get career information.

 think about it

Think about the types of jobs you want and how to find more information about them. Answer these questions.

1. Do you have a clear idea of what jobs you really want? Give some examples.

_____

_____

_____

_____

_____

2. Which jobs do you need to find out more about? (Think about earnings, working conditions, benefits, and other details.) List the information you need to find.

_____

_____

_____

_____

_____

3. How can you find more information about jobs that interest you? List some resources you have learned about. (After you list them, go out and *use* them!)

_____

_____

_____

_____

_____

PREPARE AN EFFECTIVE RESUME

An important part of the job search process is preparing a resume that details your qualifications for a particular job. It should leave a favorable impression on your potential employer.

Resumes should include your name and contact information, a clearly defined job objective (see Chapter 16), education and training, and work experience. In addition, you may want to list specific qualifications or skills, activities, interests, and references.

The Three Basic Types of Resumes

There are many types of resumes. The three most useful types of resumes are

- *The Chronological Resume:* Most resumes use this format in which the most recent experience is listed first, followed by each previous job. This format works fine for someone with work experience in several similar jobs, but not as well for those with limited experience or for career changers.

- *The Skills Resume:* The skills resume is sometimes called a functional resume. In this format, your experience is organized under key skills. A skills resume should emphasize skills that your job objective requires—those that you are good at and want to use. This format works well if you have limited work experience.

- *The Combination Resume:* A combination resume includes elements of both the chronological and skills formats. Use this type of resume if you have a good work history, but want to emphasize other life experiences besides work to support your skills.

Lisa M. Rhodes
813 Lava Court • Denver, CO 81613
Home: (413) 643-2173 (leave message)
Cell: (413) 442-1659
lrhodes@netcom.net

Objective
Sales-oriented position in a retail sales or distribution business.

Skills and Abilities

Communications	Good written and verbal presentation skills. Use proper grammar and have a good speaking voice.
Interpersonal Skills	Able to get along well with coworkers and accept supervision. Received positive evaluations from previous supervisors.
Flexible	Willing to try new things and am interested in improving efficiency on assigned tasks.
Attention to Detail	Concerned with quality. Produce work that is orderly and attractive. Ensure tasks are completed correctly and on time.
Hardworking	Throughout high school, worked long hours in strenuous activities while attending school full-time. Often managed as many as 65 hours a week in school and other structured activities while maintaining above-average grades.
Customer Service	Routinely handled as many as 500 customer contacts a day (10,000 per month) in a busy retail outlet. Averaged lower than a .001% complaint rate and was given the "Employee of the Month" award in second month of employment. Received two merit increases.
Cash Sales	Handled more than $2,000 a day ($40,000 a month) in cash sales. Balanced register and prepared daily sales summary and deposits.
Reliable	Excellent attendance record; trusted to deliver daily cash deposits totaling more than $40,000 a month.

Education
Franklin High School, 2001–2004. Classes included advanced English. Member of award-winning band. Excellent attendance record. Superior communication skills. Graduated in top 30% of class.

Other
Active gymnastics competitor for four years. Learned discipline, teamwork, how to follow instructions, and hard work. Ambitious, outgoing, reliable, and have solid work ethic.

Quick Resume Writing Tips

Following are some general guidelines for writing your resume:

- *Write it yourself.* It's okay to look at other resumes for ideas, but write your own yourself. It will force you to organize your thoughts and background.

- *Make it error-free.* One spelling or grammar error will create a negative impression. Get someone else to review your final draft for any errors. Then review it again!

- *Make it look good.* Poor copy quality, cheap paper, bad type quality, or anything else that creates a poor appearance will turn off employers. Get professional help with design and printing if necessary. Most print shops can do it all for you.

- *Be brief, be relevant.* Many good resumes fit on one page, and few justify more than two. Include only the most important points. Use short sentences and action words. If it doesn't relate to and support your job objective, cut it!

- *Be honest.* Don't overstate your qualifications. Most employers will see right through it and not hire you. If you end up getting a job you can't handle, it will *not* be to your advantage.

- *Be positive.* Emphasize your accomplishments and results. This is no place to be too humble or to display your faults.

- *Be specific.* Rather than saying "I'm good with people," say, "I supervised four people in the warehouse and increased productivity by 30 percent." Use numbers whenever possible, such as the number of people served, percentage that sales increased, or amount of dollars saved.

DEVELOP A PORTFOLIO

A portfolio can accompany a resume and enable you to showcase your work. Certain types of jobs may require that you submit a portfolio—samples of your work—to be considered for a position. This is typical for creative positions such as a graphic designer or photographer.

However, developing a portfolio can be useful in your search for many other types of jobs as well, because it can provide concrete examples of your skills. Some items you may include in a portfolio consist of awards or certificates; letters or e-mails of commendation; and flyers, bulletins, or presentations you have created.

As you complete projects at work, assemble your portfolio so that it will be ready if you need to find another job. You may also consider including portfolio documents or other work samples on a Web site, and providing the Web site address to potential employers.

think about it

Think about what you have learned about a preparing a resume and portfolio. Answer these questions.

1. How can a resume or portfolio make your job search more effective?

_____

_____

_____

_____

2. What information should you include on your resume?

_____

_____

_____

_____

3. What types of documents or other items would you include in a portfolio?

_____

_____

_____

_____

INTRODUCING THE JIST CARD®

Another important technique for making your job search more effective is called the JIST Card. A JIST Card is like a small resume. It is only three inches high by five inches long, like an index card. But with this small card, you can give people a lot of information about yourself.

Elements of a JIST Card

Here is a sample JIST Card with all its parts identified.

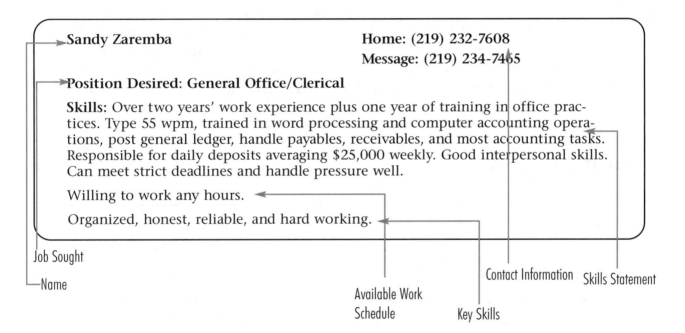

Uses of a JIST Card

During your job search, you can use your JIST Card in these ways:

- Attach one to an application when you fill it out, or attach one to your resume.

- Take it along on interviews and leave it with employers.

- Give a JIST Card to everyone in your network.

- Ask people in your network to pass your cards on to people they know.

- Leave one with employers who won't let you fill out an application or give you an interview. (When they read your JIST Card, they might change their minds.)

- Send a JIST Card along with a thank-you note after you have an interview.

Producing Your JIST Card

If your handwriting is good, you can hand-write your JIST Card. A better approach is to have it printed on a laser printer or at a copy store. Have yours neatly typed or word processed.

> ### FOCUS
> *Your JIST Card should make a good impression and be free of errors.*

Make sure that you have checked your JIST Card for errors. Mistakes give people the impression that you are sloppy or careless. Let a friend you trust read it to make sure that it is clear and effective.

When you're sure that the card is exactly right, have several hundred printed or photocopied. If you have access to a computer printer, you can print four or more JIST Cards on one sheet of light card stock. These can be cut to size after printing. Most copy or print shops also will be able to do this for you at a reasonable cost.

Sample JIST Cards

John Kijek Home: (219) 232-9213
Message: (219) 637-6643

Position Desired: Auto Mechanic

Skills: Over three years' work experience, including one year in a full-time training program. Familiar with all hand tools and most computer diagnostic techniques. Can handle common repairs such as tune-ups, brakes, exhaust systems, electrical and mechanical repairs. Am a fast worker, often completing job in less than standard time. Have all tools and can start work immediately.

Prefer full-time work, any shift.

Honest, reliable, good with people.

Juanita Rodriquez

Home: (639) 247-1643
Message: (639) 361-1754

Position Desired: Warehouse Management

Skills: Six years' experience plus two years of formal business coursework. Have supervised a staff as large as 16 people and warehousing operations covering over two acres and valued at over $14,000,000. Automated inventory operations, resulting in a 30% increase in turnover and estimated annual savings of over $250,000. Working knowledge of accounting, computer systems, time and motion studies, and advanced inventory. Will work any hours.

Responsible, hard working, and can solve problems.

Self-motivated, dependable, learn quickly.

Richard Smith

Home: (602) 253-9678
Answering Service: (602) 257-6643

Objective: Electronics installation, maintenance, and sales

Skills: Four years' work experience plus two-year associate degree in Electronics Engineering Technology. Managed a $300,000/yr. business while going to school full time, with grades in the top 25%. Familiar with all major electronics diagnostic and repair equipment. Good problem-solving and communications skills. Customer service oriented.

Willing to do what it takes to get the job done.

Energetic, dependable, learn quickly.

This chapter explained how to identify the jobs you want and how to make your job search more effective. In Chapter 8, you'll learn about one of the two best ways to find a job—getting leads from people who you already know.

think about it

Think about what you have learned about a JIST Card and the information it should include. Answer these questions.

1. How can a JIST Card make your job search more effective?

   _____

   _____

   _____

   _____

   _____

2. What information should you include on your JIST Card?

   _____

   _____

   _____

   _____

   _____

3. Name some ways to use your JIST Card.

   _____

   _____

   _____

   _____

   _____

checkpoint

After completing this chapter, answer these questions. They will help you review what you just learned.

1. How has this chapter helped you prepare for your job search?

_____

_____

_____

_____

2. Do the Challenge below. Was writing your JIST Card easy or not so easy for you? Why?

_____

_____

_____

_____

_____

challenge: Develop Your JIST Card

Make your own JIST Card. Rewrite it as many times as you need to, so that you get it just right. Get the opinion of someone you trust (such as your instructor, a former teacher, or a friend) about how you might make it better.

Check with a local print shop for prices to have your JIST Card printed. If you type it up yourself, the printing should not be very expensive.

chapter 8 _____

One of the Two Best Job Search Methods—Getting Leads from People You Know

THE GOALS OF THIS CHAPTER ARE

- To learn about the best method of searching for a job—getting job leads from people you know

- To increase your contacts by building a job search network

WARM CONTACTS: THE MOST EFFECTIVE JOB SEARCH METHOD

You now know that most jobs are not advertised. A minority of job seekers get their jobs from help wanted ads and employment agencies. The rest of the jobs are in the "hidden" job market.

How do you find these jobs? People use two methods. The first is through people they know. The second is by contacting an employer directly. You will begin learning about the first method in this chapter.

About 40 percent of all people find their jobs through someone they know. This is the most effective job search method.

Since these job leads come from our friends, relatives, and other people we know, we call this approach using "warm contacts." Later in the book, you will learn how to get job leads from people you do not know. These contacts, who are directly involved in the job field you want to be in, are called "cold contacts."

> ## FOCUS
>
> *Making contact with people you know is the best way to find a job.*

DEVELOP A NETWORK OF PEOPLE YOU KNOW

When you want to find a job, you need job leads. You can find job leads by starting a job search network.

A network starts when you talk to people you know and do the following:

- You tell them that you are looking for a job.
- You talk about what kind of job you want.
- You explain what kinds of things you can do on a job.
- You ask people you know to give you names of people they know.
- You get names of people who might hire you or who you can talk to about finding a job.

When you get the name of a person to talk to about a job, you contact that person. You call him or her on the telephone. This is also a "warm contact."

EXAMPLE

Mike Starts His Network

Read the story about Mike to see how he gets a job lead from a warm contact.

Mike is walking down the sidewalk. He runs into his friend Chris. They shake hands and sit down on a bench.

Mike: Hey, how are you doing, Chris?

Chris: Okay. How about you?

Mike: Pretty good, but I've been out of work for a while.

Chris: Oh, yeah? Maybe you should talk to Frank down at Whitman's Grocery. I've known Frank for years. He's the manager down there.

Mike: You think he might be hiring?

Chris: I was just talking to him about that the other day. I know he's got a job opening, and I think you've got the right skills and experience. Check it out. Tell him Chris sent you.

Mike: Hey, thanks Chris. And in the meantime, if you talk to other people who might have openings that I'm qualified for, could you tell them about me?

By talking to Chris, Mike has started building his network. Chris will tell his other friends about Mike. In a very short time, a growing number of people will know that Mike is looking for a job.

Mike can tell other friends that he is looking for a job. If they all tell their friends, think about how many people will be contacted. A network can grow very fast.

WHO IS IN A NETWORK?

There are many kinds of people besides friends who can be part of your network. Relatives, neighbors, and people you used to work with are some examples.

EXAMPLE

Mike's Growing Network

If you think about it, you already know many people. Read how Mike continues to build his network of job search contacts.

- Mike used to work at a shipyard. He tells people he knows there that he is looking for a job. They tell people they know.

- Mike plays baseball in a local league. He tells people he sees there that he is looking for a job. They tell people they know.

- Mike goes to church on Sundays. He tells the people he knows at his church that he is looking for a job. They tell people they know.

Here are some more people Mike includes in his network:

- People he knows at the hospital, where he volunteers.

- The parents of his friends (who tell their friends, co-workers, and so on).

- His own parents (who tell their friends, co-workers, and so on).

- People he knows in the neighborhood where he lives.

Like Mike, you can learn to develop your own network. "Develop Your Networking Skills," the Challenge at the end of Chapter 9, will show you how.

This chapter explained what a network is, and it told you how to build your network to include some people you might not have thought about.

In the next chapter, you learn how to expand your network, including how to target certain groups for your network. The chapter shows how your network can work for you, even if you're somewhere else!

checkpoint

After completing this chapter, answer these questions. They will help you review what you just learned.

1. What is a warm contact?

_____

_____

_____

_____

_____

2. How did Mike start building a network?

_____

_____

_____

_____

_____

3. Why do employers like to hire people who are recommended by someone they know?

_____

_____

_____

_____

_____

challenge: Understand Why Networking Works

Understanding an employer's point of view is a valuable skill for your job search. Use this activity to explore why using a network is so important to both you and employers.

Imagine for a moment that you are Frank, the manager at Whitman's Grocery. You (Frank) want to avoid placing an ad and taking a lot of time for interviews. You also want to hire someone you can trust.

Let's say that two people came to interview for a job. One of those people is someone you don't know. The other person is Mike, a friend of Chris's. Chris sent Mike to you and told you that he thought that Mike would be a good worker. (You've known Chris for years.) Both Mike and the other applicant seem qualified for the job.

If you were Frank, which person would you feel better about hiring? Explain why on the lines here.

_____

_____

_____

_____

_____

chapter 9

The Network in Action

THE GOALS OF THIS CHAPTER ARE

- To target people for your network
- To see how networking brings results
- To learn how to get referrals

BUILD YOUR JOB SEARCH NETWORK

This chapter helps you get started on building your own job search network. It will also teach you how to get referrals from people you know. This will make your network even larger.

You probably know lots of people and more than you realize. Some of them you know well and some not so well. This section will help you list the people you know. And each one knows other people. All these people can become your own job search network.

List Your Friends

Start building your network by making a list of your friends. Not just close friends. Include anyone you can think of who is friendly with you.

List of Friends

Write friends' names in the left column. In the right column, make a note of how you will contact that person. If you always run into that person at a certain place, write that down. If you plan to call on the telephone, use the space to write in the person's telephone number. Use an extra sheet of paper if you run out of room.

Person's Name   **How I Can Make Contact**

_____   _____

_____   _____

_____   _____

_____   _____

_____   _____

_____   _____

_____   _____

_____   _____

List Other People You Know

There are many more people besides friends to include in your network. The list that follows will give you ideas for the groups of people you know. Look it over. Put a check mark by each group that makes sense for you. Then use the extra lines to add other groups that are not on the list.

You may not know some people in these groups very well. That doesn't matter for now. There are many different groups of people to target for your network. Can you add any to this list?

Relatives

Fellow church members

Parents of friends

Neighbors

Co-workers

Members of clubs

People who sell you things

Former employers

People you know through sports

Guidance counselors

_____

_____

_____

_____

_____

_____

List of Other Contacts

Now do the same thing that you did with your list of friends. Write down the names of every person you know in each group checked above and how you plan to make contact.

Put a check mark beside each name every time you talk to that person about a job lead. In the "Date Contacted" column, fill in the date you talked. This way, you can follow up on contacts you made earlier.

Before you begin writing on the worksheet that follows, copy it several times. Soon you may have dozens of people to contact. Or even hundreds. Once you begin contacting people, you can use these lists to keep track of your contacts.

Person's Name	How I Can Make Contact	Date Contacted
_____	_____	_____
_____	_____	_____
_____	_____	_____
_____	_____	_____
_____	_____	_____
_____	_____	_____
_____	_____	_____
_____	_____	_____

```
_____    _____    _____

_____    _____    _____

_____    _____
```

think about it

Think about the concept of networking and how you can target people for your network. Answer these questions.

1. Why is building your network important to your job search? Explain.

_____

_____

_____

_____

_____

2. Explain why it is important to keep a list of the contacts you make. Write your reasons on the lines below.

_____

_____

_____

_____

_____

EXAMPLE

How Mike's Network Works for Him

In Chapter 8, you saw how Mike began to build his network. You should have also started thinking about who you will include in your own network.

It might seem to you that there is a lot of talking going on in Mike's network. But you may wonder, where is the action? What happens next? Read on! You'll soon find out.

Mrs. Brown (Mike's mother) is on her coffee break at work. Sandra Parker, another employee, is at the table in the employee lounge with her. They are talking.

Mrs. Brown: Did I tell you my son Mike is looking for work?

Mrs. Parker: Why didn't you say so before? My neighbor Sam mentioned just the other day that he needs a good worker down at his office.

Mrs. Brown: Do you have his telephone number?

Mrs. Parker: I'll call you this evening and tell you what it is. Have Mike give Sam a call. I'll tell Sam all about him.

That evening, Mrs. Parker gives Mike's mother the telephone number. Mike calls Sam the next morning. They schedule a meeting for later in the week. Mike has an interview! Meanwhile, another part of Mike's network is busy, too.

Barb Riley is a friend of Mike's girlfriend. Barb works at a shipping company. She is having a meeting with her boss. Her boss, Sheila Danville, interrupts the meeting to take a telephone call.

Sheila (frowning): You said Jones quit? Just walked off the job? Oh, for crying out loud. Why can't we find workers we can trust? Well, okay. Do the best you can. (She hangs up the phone.)

Barb: Trouble, Sheila?

Sheila: Oh, somebody just left us in the lurch down at the loading dock. He's one of the guys I hired from that want ad we placed last month. I knew we were taking a chance with him.

Barb: Well, I happen to know a guy who is looking for a job right now. I've known him for a long time, Sheila, and I guarantee that he's reliable.

Sheila: Tell him to give me a call. Right away!

On her lunch break, Barb calls Mike's girlfriend. Mike's girlfriend calls Mike and gives him Sheila's telephone number. Mike calls Sheila, and they set up a meeting for the next day. Mike has another interview!

A NETWORK CAN WORK FOR YOU

In the previous examples, Mike got two job leads from people in his network. He didn't expect these job leads. He didn't find them himself. These jobs were not advertised. There was no other way he could have found out about them.

That is how the hidden job market works. The more people who are helping you look, the better. One of them will find out about a job opening. If that person is in your network, he or she will think of you. It's that simple.

 think about it

Think about how the hidden job market benefited Mike in the previous examples. Answer these questions.

1. How did Mike benefit from the hidden job market?

   _____

   _____

   _____

   _____

2. Why did Sheila want to talk to Mike?

   _____

   _____

   _____

   _____

HOW TO GET REFERRALS FROM YOUR NETWORK

You have seen three examples of how Mike's network is working:

- Mike talked to his friend Chris → Chris sent Mike to Frank, who manages a grocery store.

- Mike talked to his mother → Mike's mother talked to a co-worker, Sandra Parker → Mrs. Parker knew of a job opening with her neighbor, Sam → Mike called Sam.

- Mike's girlfriend talked to her friend, Barb Riley → Barb talked to her boss, Sheila Danville → Mike called Sheila Danville.

In each of these examples, Mike got referrals. A *referral* is the name of someone to talk to. Chris referred Mike to Frank. Mrs. Parker referred Mike to Sam. Barb Riley referred Mike to Sheila Danville.

Every time you talk to one of your warm contacts, try to get at least two referrals.

EXAMPLE

How Mike Gets Referrals

Mike has just finished his volunteer work at the hospital. He is in the employee locker room, gathering his things into his duffel bag before he leaves to go home. Dan Martinez, a guy Mike works with, is nearby.

Dan: So Mike, how's the job hunt going?

Mike: Oh, I've been talking to a lot of people. And I've been meaning to ask you about that. Do you know anyone who has a job opening in the kind of work I do?

Dan: No, I don't know of a job opening. But I know someone who might have an opening later on.

Mike gets the person's name, company name, and telephone number from Dan.

Mike: This is great, Dan. Thanks. Can you think of anybody else?

Dan: Off the top of my head, I can think of one more person you could call. He probably doesn't have an opening, but he might know someone else who does. And I'll tell you what, Mike. I'll keep thinking about it, and when I have some more names, I'll call you.

Mike: I really appreciate it, Dan.

Mike got two referrals from Dan, and he might get more.

THREE QUESTIONS TO ASK WHEN GETTING REFERRALS

When you are talking to your warm contacts about your job search, be sure to ask the following three questions one at a time. If the first question gets you a referral, write down the name and phone number. Then ask the second question. If you still haven't received two names, then ask the third question.

The three questions are as follows. Do you...

- Know of anyone who might have a job opening in my field?
- Know of anyone who might know someone who has a job opening in my field?
- Know someone who knows a lot of people?

Most people may not be able to give you a name for the first or even the second question. It is important to keep asking the questions until you get the referrals.

This chapter wrapped up one of the best job search methods—using people you already know as contacts. The next chapter introduces the other best way to find a job—contacting employers directly.

 checkpoint

After completing this chapter, answer these questions. They will help you review what you just learned.

1. What is a referral?

_____

_____

_____

_____

2. How are referrals important to your job search?

_____

_____

_____

_____

3. What are the three questions to ask when you are getting referrals?

_____

_____

_____

_____

challenge: Develop Your Networking Skills

Call three people from the network lists you put together. Ask each of these people the three questions you learned for getting referrals. Keep notes of any information the three people give you in the space here.

_____

_____

_____

_____

_____

Another of the Best Job Search Methods—Direct Contact with Employers

THE GOALS OF THIS CHAPTER ARE

- To learn about the second best method for finding a job—making direct contact with employers who could use your skills

- To learn how to make direct contacts with employers and other people you do not know

MOVING FROM "WARM" TO "COLD"

You have learned to find job leads from people you know. We called these warm contacts. You used warm contacts to build your network.

You will now learn about getting job leads by making cold contacts. These are contacts you make directly with employers. You do not know these people. That is why these are called "cold" contacts.

FOCUS
These methods might make you nervous, but they work.

THE TWO MOST COMMON WAYS TO MAKE COLD CONTACTS

- Call a company or organization on the telephone.
- Drop in without an appointment.

Calling a company on the phone or dropping in without an appointment might make you feel nervous. But many people have used these methods to get interviews.

Next to warm contacts, making direct contacts with employers is the most effective job search method. Almost 30 percent of all people get their jobs this way. This is twice as effective as answering want ads.

FIND EMPLOYERS WHO NEED YOU

Looking for a job can be lonely. When you are out of work, it seems like everyone in the world is at work but you.

You might live in a small town or a large city. Wherever you live, everywhere you go, you see people working. Everyone seems to have a place to go and something to do. Everyone, that is, but you.

The truth is, you have a place, too! Somewhere, there is a job that is right for you. Somewhere, there is an employer who needs you. You might find that job and that employer through your job search network.

But that is only half of your job search. The other half is to actively contact employers who may never know you exist—until you tell them!

THE YELLOW PAGES—A LARGE LISTING OF POTENTIAL EMPLOYERS

A large listing of employers is one reason that the yellow pages is a great resource for job seekers. You have an almost-complete listing of employers in your area, right at your fingertips.

There is another reason the yellow pages is a good place to start. It has an index, which organizes all the businesses and services into groups, or categories. The index makes it fast and easy for you to locate the types of jobs that interest you.

Get a copy of your local yellow pages. Then find the index section. The index is usually in the front section of the book.

> ### FOCUS
>
> *Somewhere, there is an employer who needs you.*

Using the Yellow Pages

Let's look at a yellow pages example. Notice that some of the lines are in bold type. These are categories. The categories are listed in alphabetical order. Products and services are then listed under each category.

To complete this worksheet, use the sample below and the index of your yellow pages.

1. Imagine that you need an accountant. To find one, you go to the yellow pages index. Find the word "Accountants" in the example above and circle it.

2. "Accountants" is in bold type. It is the name of a category. Under "Accountants" there is a list of words in lighter type. On the lines below, write these words and the numbers that appear next to them.

_____

_____

The words you just wrote are types of accounting services. The numbers next to them are the page numbers where you will find each one.

3. Now try locating something in your own yellow pages. Say you want to find information about vocational education. Find "Vocational" in the index.

(continued)

(continued)

You may have to look up several categories to find what you want. In this example, you could also look under the category "Schools."

4. On the lines below, list all the headings in regular type under the word "Vocational." Also list the page numbers that appear next to them.

_____

_____

5. Look at the first heading you listed in item 5. In your yellow pages directory, turn to the page number you wrote down.

6. Write the names, addresses, and telephone numbers of three of the services you find.

_____

_____

EXAMPLE

Maria Uses the Yellow Pages to Find Job Leads

Read the story that follows to see how Maria Cortez used the yellow pages to find job leads.

Maria is looking for a job. She once worked on a construction crew. She learned how to work with certain kinds of equipment. Maria liked the job. She would like to find another one like it.

Maria turned to the yellow pages index. She looked under "C" for Construction.

Using a pencil, Maria put a check mark beside the headings that interested her. Then she wrote down the page numbers of each of those headings. She wrote them in a notebook that she had labeled "job prospects."

Maria turned to the page that listed "Building Contractors." In her job prospects notebook, she wrote the names and telephone numbers of all the companies she wanted to contact about jobs she could do.

Maria did this for each heading she had checked off in the index. Soon she had a long list of companies to call.

GETTING EVEN MORE LEADS

Maria looked under "Construction" since she was interested in these jobs. And she found some good leads. But here is a way you can find many more job leads.

Look at every listing in the index. As you do, ask yourself, "Would this type of organization be able to use a person with my skills?" If the answer is "yes," then mark that listing. Use the system that follows:

- Write "1" if that organization sounds interesting to you.

- Write "2" if you are not sure.

- Write "3" if that organization does not sound interesting to you.

If Maria did this, one of the many listings she would find would be "Hospitals." This type of organization could use her skills. So she would then mark that listing. Let's say that she marked it with a "1" because it sounded interesting.

Later, she could contact the hospitals and try to get a job using her construction and building repair skills. In the next chapter, you will see how Maria learned to make telephone calls to these employers.

 checkpoint

After completing this chapter, answer these questions. They will help you review what you just learned.

1. Describe how the yellow pages index is organized.

_____

_____

_____

_____

_____

2. What are two reasons why the yellow pages is an excellent resource for finding job leads?

_____

_____

_____

_____

_____

challenge: Find Employers to Contact

Begin your job prospects notebook, like Maria's. Use the yellow pages index to locate possible employers. Then put the names, addresses, and telephone numbers in your notebook. Keep track of who you contact, and when.

How many prospects do you have? What have you learned in starting your job prospects notebook? Answer these questions and add any related thoughts on the lines below.

_____

_____

_____

_____

_____

_____

_____

_____

_____

chapter 11

Telephone and Employer Contact Skills

THE GOALS OF THIS CHAPTER ARE

- To learn good telephone skills for making cold contacts effectively
- To learn other contact skills that you will use in your job search

GETTING YOUR FOOT IN THE DOOR

To get a job, you need to be able to communicate. You need to let people know who you are and what you can do.

And, of course, you need to get interviews with people who can hire you. To get interviews, you need to know how to get your foot in the door at organizations that might be able to use your skills.

Read on to learn more ways to make your contact with possible employers successful. For more detailed information on the interview process, refer to Part 4 of this book.

MAKING TELEPHONE CONTACT WITH EMPLOYERS

When you are ready to call a possible employer, keep two goals in mind:

- Get to the person who supervises people with your skills.
- Get an interview.

GETTING TO THE PERSON WHO SUPERVISES

When you are contacting an employer for the first time, you will need to get the name of a person to talk to about a job in your field, the best time to call that person, and the person's job title (for example, supervisor, foreman, manager).

This sounds fairly simple, and often it is. But it can sometimes present a problem. That's because job seekers might be sent to the company's personnel department.

What Is a Personnel Department?

One of the main jobs of a personnel department (sometimes called a human resources or "HR" department) is to find good employees. There is, however, another critical job for the personnel department. It is to screen out job applicants. If your application does not look just right, your application will often be rejected.

Why You Should Avoid the Personnel Department

About two out of three people now work in small organizations (250 or fewer employees). Most of these companies are not large enough to have a separate personnel department.

Even many big organizations don't have personnel departments. You want to get to the person who will supervise you. This person is the one who will make a decision to hire you. That is why getting to the supervisor is your first goal in contacting an employer.

The sample telephone script that appears later in this chapter will help you avoid being steered to the personnel department.

GETTING AN INTERVIEW

Your other goal in contacting an employer is to get an interview. An interview is a meeting you have with an employer to discuss what the job is and why you are qualified to do it (see Part 4 for more information).

In Chapter 10, you saw how Maria Cortez made a list of employers to call from the yellow pages. Now you can read how she accomplishes the two goals of making contact on the telephone.

EXAMPLE

Maria Gathers Information for Contacting Possible Employers

Maria looks at the list she made of job prospects. She dials the number of the first company on her list. A receptionist answers the telephone.

Receptionist: A and B Builders. May I help you?

Maria: Hi. I'm looking for a job, and I'd like to talk to someone about that.

Receptionist: I'll direct your call to the personnel department. Hold, please, while I transfer you.

The person Maria talks to in the personnel department tells her to come in and fill out an application. Did Maria get to the person who could supervise her? No. What could she have done differently? Maria tries again, this time with the second company on her list.

Receptionist: Good morning. This is Jones Contracting. May I help you?

Maria: Hi. Could I speak with the person who supervises your building crews?

Receptionist: What is the nature of your call, please?

Maria: I am looking for a job.

Receptionist: I'll transfer your call to personnel.

Whoops! It happened again. How can Maria get the name of someone to talk to outside of the personnel department? She tries again.

Maria: Hello. My name is Maria Cortez. I'd like the name of the person who supervises the construction crews.

Receptionist: What is the nature of your call?

Maria: I have some information to send this person, and I'd like to get the correct spelling of the name and the address.

Receptionist: His name is John O'Keefe. The address is 9101 Market Street, ZIP code 44502.

Maria: Mr. O'Keefe's telephone number would be helpful, too.

(continued)

(continued)

Receptionist: His extension is 381.

Maria: If I should need to contact him by telephone, when is the best time to reach him?

Receptionist: He is usually in the office in the mornings between 8 and 10. After that he is in and out a lot.

Maria: Thanks very much. I appreciate your help.

This time, Maria got the information she needed. What did she do that was different from the first two calls she made? The next "Think About It" will help you answer that question.

 ## think about it

Fill in the blanks and answer the questions that follow.

1. Maria asked for the _____
   (job title) of a group of workers.

2. Before making the call, Maria decided to ask for a specific area of the company, which was _____
   (the type of work done by those workers).

3. When the receptionist asked Maria why she was calling, Maria did not say she was looking for a job. Instead, she said she needed the supervisor's name so that she could do what?

   _____

   _____

   _____

4. After she got the supervisor's name and address, what else did Maria ask for?

   _____

   _____

   _____

5. What other information did Maria get that would help her contact Mr. O'Keefe?

_____

_____

_____

6. At the end of their conversation, Maria remembered to _____ _____ the receptionist for the information.

TIPS FOR MAKING TELEPHONE CONTACTS

When you are using the telephone to contact an employer, follow these tips:

- Be courteous.

- Give your name and sound professional.

- Get the name of someone in charge of jobs that you would like to have (not someone in the personnel department).

- Find a way to state your business without saying you are looking for a job. (For example, "I have some business to discuss," or "I have some information I believe will interest him or her.")

- Get the person's telephone number, business address, or both.

- Thank the receptionist—you may be speaking with that person again!

- If you reach a voice-mail system, try to connect with an operator and follow the tips above.

KEEP CALLING UNTIL YOU GET THROUGH

You might not always get through to the person you want to reach. There will be times when the best you will get is a transfer to the personnel department. Or the receptionist might refuse to give you the name of someone unless you state exactly why you are calling.

But most of the time, you will find people who are willing to help you. So keep trying, and don't be discouraged by the ones who screen you out.

> ## FOCUS
>
> *Practice your cold calls. It will make you less nervous.*

EXAMPLE

Maria Practices Telephone Contacts

Maria used the yellow pages to find employers. She made calls to find the names of people to contact. Now she is ready to call Mr. O'Keefe.

Maria is very nervous. She does not like calling people she does not know. She is afraid she will say the wrong thing or sound as nervous as she feels.

Tom Duncan, Maria's friend, has recently been through the job search process himself. He knows how Maria feels. Tom suggests to Maria that they practice calling an employer together. He will pose as an employer. Maria can then rehearse what she is going to say.

Maria pretends to call Mr. O'Keefe on the telephone. Tom poses as Mr. O'Keefe, answering the telephone.

Maria: May I speak with Mr. O'Keefe, please?

Tom: This is Mr. O'Keefe.

Maria: Hello. My name is Maria Cortez. I am interested in a position on one of your construction crews. I would like to meet with you to tell you about my skills and experience.

Tom: Well, go ahead and send me your resume, and I'll take a look at it.

Maria: I'd be happy to send you my resume, but I'd really like to set up an appointment with you at your convenience.

Tom: I don't have any actual job openings right now, Ms. Cortez.

Maria: I see. I know you must be very busy, but I'd like to bring my resume to you in person and spend a few minutes talking with you. That way, if you should need a person with my skills later on, you'll already know something about me.

Tom: That sounds like a good idea. Can you come to my office Wednesday at 9 a.m.?

Maria: That sounds fine. Thank you very much.

Maria continued to practice until she felt confident enough to make the real call to Mr. O'Keefe. When she did, she got an interview.

This won't always work. If the person is too busy or unwilling to see you, politely end the call. Don't get discouraged. Keep trying other contacts.

think about it

Think about ways to contact key personnel at companies where you would like to work. Answer these questions.

1. What are the two goals to keep in mind when you make contact with a possible employer?

_____

_____

_____

_____

_____

2. Why is it best to avoid the personnel department? (Who should you try to contact instead?)

_____

_____

_____

_____

_____

3. List several tips for making telephone contact with possible employers.

_____

_____

_____

_____

_____

DROP IN ON EMPLOYERS

You have learned skills to locate employers who might hire you and to make contact with them. You can use these same skills in an even more direct way than calling on the telephone. Stopping by a place of business or an organization without an appointment is okay.

FOCUS
It's okay to stop by a business without an appointment.

Some employers will be willing to see you on short notice. For those who can't see you, the visit can still be worthwhile if you do the following:

- Ask to make an appointment for another day.

- Leave your JIST Card and resume with the receptionist, and ask that they be passed on to the appropriate person.

- Gather information about the organization and the job.

 checkpoint

After completing this chapter, answer these questions. They will help you review what you just learned.

1. If you want a job as an editor at a magazine, who might you ask for when contacting the employer by phone?

_____

_____

_____

_____

_____

2. Why is "dropping in" on a possible employer worthwhile?

_____

_____

_____

_____

_____

 # CHALLENGE: Develop Your Employer Contact Skills

Practicing skills helps you build confidence. The activity that follows can help you make your contacts with possible employers more effective.

Write a telephone script to use as practice for making telephone calls to possible employers. Keep it short and write the way you talk.

Your script should include the following:

- Your name
- Why you are calling
- A statement about your skills and what makes you a good worker

You can use your JIST Card as the basis for a phone script. Your script should end with the question, "When may I come in for an interview?"

Write your script in the following space. Use extra pages if needed.

_____

_____

_____

_____

_____

CONCLUSION: FIND A BETTER JOB IN LESS TIME

An effective job search should use a variety of job search methods. Feel free to use any job search method you want, but just be sure to spend most of your time using the two methods that are more effective for most people—getting leads from people you already know, and making direct contacts with employers.

We hope that the information in Part 2 has helped you learn how to find a better job in less time.

Part 3

Introduction to Job Applications

- Chapter 12: Application Basics
- Chapter 13: Gather Information for Your Application
- Chapter 14: How to Use an Application in Your Job Search
- Chapter 15: Practice with Applications

How many times have you started a project, only to find that you don't have the tool you need to complete it? Projects can come to a halt until you get the right wrench, a smaller paintbrush, or a bigger measuring cup. Maybe you have the right tool, but you don't know how to use it. Anyone can buy tools to tune a piano, for example, but without knowledge and training the tools won't help.

Before you start your job search, you should learn about the tools available to help you. Some tools are better than others. Filling out application forms is *not* one of the better tools. (Later, we'll explain why.)

However, most employers require you to fill out an application before they will consider hiring you. So since you have to do it anyway, it's a good idea to learn how to make applications work for you, not against you. That's what you'll learn to do in Part 3 of this book.

Applications can be confusing. Many people have problems filling out job applications. Preparation and practice can avoid those problems. In Part 3 you will learn about the following:

- Why employers use applications and what kind of information they want to know.
- Problems to avoid when filling out applications.
- How to increase your chances of being considered for the job you want.

With this information, you will have a better chance of standing out and getting the job you want.

chapter 12

Application Basics

THE GOALS OF THIS CHAPTER ARE

- To understand why employers use applications
- To learn how applications can be an obstacle to getting a job

WHAT IS AN APPLICATION FORM?

An application form provides an employer with information about you. Employers need this information to see whether you are the right person for the job they need to fill.

WHY EMPLOYERS USE APPLICATIONS

Imagine that you work for a busy company. You are in charge of hiring new workers. You have 3 job openings now and about 50 people are applying for each job.

You need to fill the jobs as quickly as possible. What's the fastest way to get through 150 job applicants to find the 3 best ones?

Employers can look through a stack of 150 job applications much more quickly than they can talk to 150 people. In fact, many applicants will be ruled out after a quick glance at their applications. This is a process for screening out as many applicants as possible.

Application forms are designed to help an employer quickly spot an applicant's inexperience and other weaknesses. An employer does this to eliminate all but the most qualified applicants.

KEY PRINCIPLES TO USING AN APPLICATION

- Use your application to help make a good first impression.
- Avoid answers that can screen you out.

Employers are busy people. They need to fill job openings as quickly as possible.

Interviewing many job applicants takes time. But using application forms to screen out applicants is quick. Some employers use computerized or Internet applications. Many of the tips that apply to paper applications can be used in completing electronic applications as well. Whatever the format, remember that the employer's goal is to select workers who

- Can do the job
- Will be reliable
- Can be trusted
- Will work hard

Pages 120 and 121 show what an application form looks like. If you want, you can complete it as if you were looking for a job.

Of course, different employers use different forms. Part 3 of this book gives you the general information you'll need and a variety of sample applications for practice.

Read the following story to see how an application form can be used to screen you out.

EXAMPLE

Who Gets Screened Out?

Gary needed a job. Recently he had seen a sign on the front door of a shoe store. The sign said "Help Wanted." Gary decided to go into the store and fill out a job application.

When he got inside, he spoke with a woman behind the counter. Gary asked her what kind of job was open. The woman described the job to Gary. "Can you do a job like that?" she asked.

"I think so," Gary said. The woman handed him an application form. "Please fill out this application form. You can sit down over there," she said, pointing to a chair in a corner. Gary had nothing to write with. He had to ask the woman for a pen.

Another woman sat nearby, also filling out an application. She was wearing a nice dress and good shoes. She looked like she was ready to start working right away, if they wanted her to. She had a notebook next to her and looked at it from time to time while she wrote on the application form.

Gary sat in his chair and looked over the form the sales associate had given him. It had many small boxes with small printed letters. There wasn't much room to write in the boxes. There were questions Gary didn't understand. Gary had to leave a lot of boxes blank because he didn't have the information the form needed.

He didn't know his Social Security number or the address of the high school he had attended. He didn't know the phone numbers of his references. Gary started to fill in the information that he could. He made a mistake, so he had to cross it out. In the space that was left, he had to write so small that it was hard to read.

Gary noticed that the woman sitting nearby was closing her notebook and putting her pen into her purse. She must be finished, he thought. "I'll bet you're glad that's over, huh?" he said, to make conversation.

She looked surprised and then gave a little shrug. "Oh, it was okay. It's what I expected." She stood up. "It's just another step in the right direction for me," she said. "I'm going to manage this store someday—or another one like it." She smiled. "I know what I want."

As the woman went on her way, Gary looked back over his application. The boxes he had filled in looked messy. By the time Gary handed the form back to the woman at the counter, he felt confused and frustrated.

The woman glanced over Gary's application. "We'll call you if we need you," she said. "Okay, thanks," Gary said. But as he went out the door, he had a feeling that they weren't going to call him at all.

Bill's Dependable Co.

APPLICATION FOR EMPLOYMENT

(PLEASE PRINT REQUESTED INFORMATION IN INK)   Date _____

Bill's is an Equal Opportunity Employer and does not discriminate against any individual in any phase of employment in accordance with the requirements of local, state, and federal law. In addition, Bill's has adopted an Affirmative Action Program with the goals of ensuring equitable representation of qualified women, minorities, Vietnam Era and disabled veterans, and other disabled individuals, at all job levels.

Applicants may be subject to testing for illegal drugs. In addition, applicants for certain positions who receive a conditional offer of employment must pass a medical examination prior to receiving a confirmed offer of employment.

This application will be considered active for 60 days. If you have not been employed within this period and are still interested in employment at Bill's, please contact the office where you applied and request that your application be reactivated.

PERSONAL INFORMATION

Last Name	First Name	Middle Name	Social Security No.

Street Address	City	State	Zip Code	County	Telephone No. ( )

If hired, can you furnish proof of age? ☐ Yes ☐ No

If hired, can you furnish proof that you are legally entitled to work in the U.S.? ☐ Yes ☐ No

Answer the following questions only if the position for which you are applying requires driving.

Are you licensed to drive a car? ☐ Yes ☐ No   Is license valid in this state? ☐ Yes ☐ No

Have you ever been employed by Bill's or a subsidiary of Bill's? ☐ Yes ☐ No

If Yes, note unit number and address   Termination Date   Position

Do you have any relatives employed by Bill's in the store or unit in which you are applying? ☐ Yes ☐ No   If Yes, Name/Relationship:

In order to assure proper placement of all associates, please list any special skills, training, or experiences that qualify you for the position for which you are applying.

_____

_____

_____

AVAILABILITY

I am applying for the following position:

☐ Sales   ☐ Office   ☐ Mechanical   ☐ Merchandise Handling

☐ Other (specify)

Date you are available to start work:

I am seeking (check only one):   I am available for:

☐ Seasonal employment (one season, e.g., Christmas)   ☐ Part-time employment   ☐ Full-time employment

☐ Regular employment (employ. for indefinite period of time)   Complete the Hours Available for Work Chart Below.

If temporary, indicate dates available: _____

Total hours available per week: _____

	Mon.	Tue.	Wed.	Thur.	Fri.	Sat.	Sun.
FROM							
TO							

MISCELLANEOUS

Within the past seven years, have you been convicted of a crime involving dishonesty or violence? (A conviction record will not necessarily be a bar to employment.)

☐ Yes   ☐ No

If Yes, explain: _____

EDUCATION

	DID YOU GRADUATE?		
Names and Locations of Schools Attended	Yes	No	Course of Study
High School			
College			Major Degree
Other (name and type)			

WORK EXPERIENCE

List below your four most recent employers, starting with your present or last employer. List under company name any periods of unemployment. If you were employed under another name, please enter under the company name.

Company Name	Address & Phone	Mo./Yr.	Rate of Pay	Title of Job Held / Name of Supervisor	Reason for Leaving
		From	Starting		
		To	Final		
		From	Starting		
		To	Final		
		From	Starting		
		To	Final		
		From	Starting		
		To	Final		

PLEASE READ THE FOLLOWING PARAGRAPH BEFORE SIGNING THIS APPLICATION

I certify that the information contained in this application is correct to the best of my knowledge and understand that any misstatement or omission of information is grounds for dismissal in accordance with Bill's Dependable Co. policy. I authorize the references listed above to give you any and all information concerning my previous employment and any pertinent information they may have, personal or otherwise, and release all parties from all liability for any damages that may result from furnishing same to you. In consideration of my employment, I agree to conform to the rules and regulations of Bill's Dependable Co., and my employment and compensation can be terminated with or without cause, and with or without notice, at any time, at the option of either the Company or myself. I understand that no unit manager or representative of Bill's Dependable Co., other than an Officer of the Company, has any authority to enter into any agreement for employment for any specified period of time, or to make any agreement contrary to the foregoing. In some states, the law requires that Bill's have my written permission before obtaining consumer reports on me, and I hereby authorize Bill's to obtain such reports.

Applicant's Signature _____ Date _____

OFFICE USE ONLY

Unit Name and Number

Employment Date	Dept. or Division No.		☐ REGULAR ☐ PART-TIME
Job Title		Job Code Job Grade	
Compensation Arrangement		Associate No.	Time Card Rack No.
Authorized Signature			Date

think about it

Gary was right. This employer is not likely to call him. His application probably was "screened out" as soon as he was out the door.

Can you think of some reasons why Gary might be screened out? Write them in the space that follows.

_____

_____

_____

_____

MAKE A GOOD IMPRESSION

Nearly all large organizations and many small ones will require you to fill out an application form when you apply for a job. You'll have an advantage over most other job applicants if you use the form to make a good impression and avoid answers that can screen you out.

Appearances Count

To make hiring decisions, employers often have to rely on their first impressions. They get those impressions from the way you present information about yourself. Employers consider both the information and the way you present it. If employers don't get a good impression from your application, they won't want to interview you. They just won't want to take the time.

Remember the young woman next to Gary who was filling out an application at the same time? Gary noticed that she seemed ready to start working right away. Her appearance made a good first impression on Gary. Her appearance probably impressed the sales associate, too. If so, the sales associate might put in a good word to the employer.

First impressions make a difference. The way you look and the way your application is completed will make a difference. If you make a bad first impression, you may not be considered for the job. This is often true even if you have the skills to do the job. For this reason, you must learn to make a good first impression.

Hints for Completing Applications

Here are some good practices to follow when filling out applications. Later in this chapter we will review each one.

- Read and follow all directions carefully.

- Use an erasable black pen.

- Don't leave anything blank. Write N.A. for "does Not Apply" if something does not apply to you.

- Bring names, addresses, dates, and other information you are likely to need with you.

- Look for ways to add positive information about yourself.

- Avoid giving negative information about yourself.

- Be as neat as possible.

> **FOCUS**
>
> *Your application can help make a good first impression.*

Albert C. Smith's Less-than-Perfect Application

On the following pages is a sample application for you to look over. This application includes many mistakes. Keeping in mind what you have learned so far, see how many mistakes you can spot. On the application itself, circle each mistake you find or note anything that could be improved.

APPLICATION FOR EMPLOYMENT

PLEASE PRINT INFORMATION REQUESTED IN INK.

Date _April 1_

BROWN'S IS AN EQUAL OPPORTUNITY EMPLOYER and fully subscribes to the principles of Equal Employment Opportunity. Brown's has adopted an Affirmative Action Program to ensure that all applicants and employees are considered for hire, promotion and job status, without regard to race, color, religion, sex, national origin, age, handicap, or status as a disabled veteran or veteran of the Vietnam Era.

To protect the interests of all concerned, applicants for certain job assignments must pass a physical examination before they are hired.

Note: This application will be considered active for 90 days. If you have not been employed within this period and are still interested in employment at Brown's, please contact the office where you applied and request that your application be reactivated.

Name _Albert C. Smith_ — Last / First / Middle

Social Security Number _411- 76-2614_ (Please present your Social Security Card for review)

Address _1526 N. Otter_ — Number / Street / City / State / Zip Code

County _Marion_

Previous Address _Same_ — Number / Street / City / State / Zip Code

Current phone or nearest phone _____

Best time of day to contact _any_

(Answer only if position for which you are applying requires driving)

If hired, can you furnish proof of age? ✓ Yes ___ No

Licensed to drive car? ___ Yes ___ No

If hired, can you furnish proof that you are legally entitled to work in U.S.? ✓ Yes ___ No

Is license valid in this state? ___ Yes ___ No

Have you ever been employed by Brown's. Yes ___ No ✗ If so, when ___ Position ___

Have you a relative in the employment of Brown's Department Store? Yes ___ No ✗

A PHYSICAL OR MENTAL DISABILITY WILL NOT CAUSE REJECTION IF IN BROWN'S MEDICAL OPINION YOU ARE ABLE TO SATISFACTORILY PERFORM IN THE POSITION FOR WHICH YOU ARE BEING CONSIDERED. Alternative placement, if available, of an applicant who does not meet the physical standards of the job for which he/she was originally considered is permitted.

Do you have any physical or mental impairment which may limit your ability to perform the job for which you are applying? _Yes I have a back problem & was in Central State Hospital for 6 months_

If yes, what can reasonably be done to accommodate your limitation? _____

	School Attended	No. of Years	Name of School	City/State	Graduate?	Course or College Major	Average Grades
EDUCATION	Grammar	6	Holy Trinty	Scranton	Yes	General	B
	Jr. High	3	Best View	"	"	"	B
	Sr. High	3	WCHS	"	"	College Prep	C
	Other			"	"		
	College	3	State U	Scranton	NO		C

	Branch of Service	Date Entered Service	Date of Discharge	Highest Rank Held	Service-Related Skills and Experience Applicable to Civilian Employment
MILITARY SERVICE	USA	1995	1998	E-3	radio stuff

What experience or training have you had other than your work experience, military service and education? (Community activities, hobbies, etc.) _____

I am interested in the type of work I have checked:

Sales ✗ Office ✗ Mechanical ✗ Warehouse ✗ Other (Specify): ✓ _____

Or the following specific job _anything_

I am seeking (check only one):
- ✓ Temporary employment (6 days or less)
- ✓ Seasonal employment (one season, e.g. Christmas)
- ✓ Regular employment (employment for indefinite period of time)

I am available for (check only one)
- ✓ Part-Time
- ✓ Full-Time

If part-time, indicate maximum hours per week and enter hours available in block to the right.

If temporary, indicate dates available _____

Have you been convicted during the past seven years of a serious crime involving a person's life or property?

NO ✗ YES ___ If yes, explain: _drunk in public_

HOURS AVAILABLE FOR WORK	
Sunday	To
Monday	To
Tuesday	To _anytime_
Wednesday	To
Thursday	To
Friday	To
Saturday	To

REFERENCES

LIST BELOW YOUR FOUR MOST RECENT EMPLOYERS, BEGINNING WITH THE CURRENT OR MOST RECENT ONE. IF YOU HAVE HAD FEWER THAN FOUR EMPLOYERS, USE THE REMAINING SPACES FOR PERSONAL REFERENCES. IF YOU WERE EMPLOYED UNDER A MAIDEN OR OTHER NAME, PLEASE ENTER THAT NAME IN THE RIGHT HAND MARGIN. IF APPLICABLE, ENTER SERVICE IN THE ARMED FORCES ON THE REVERSE SIDE.

NAMES AND ADDRESSES OF FORMER EMPLOYERS BEGINNING WITH THE CURRENT OR MOST RECENT	Nature of Employer's Business	Name of Your Supervisor	What kind of work did you do?	Starting Date	Starting Pay	Date of Leaving	Pay at Leaving	Why did you leave? Give details
Name: — / Tel. No. — / Address: Walnut St. / City: Scranton State: PA Zip Code: —	School	Eric Burgess	Clean up	Month ? Year 99	$7 an hr. Per Week	Month — Present Year	Per Week	Fired
NOTE: State reason for and length of inactivity between present application date and last employer.								
Name: Fred Willis / Tel. No. — / Address: ? / City: Scranton State: PA Zip Code: —	Houses	Rafael	electrician helper laborer	Month 7 Year 98	$6.50 an hr Per Week	Month — Year	Per Week	looked for a job for almost a year
NOTE: State reason for and length of inactivity between present application date and last employer.								
Name: Wayne Constr. / Tel. No. 555-4141 / Address: 1436 N. Anderson / City: Scranton State: PA Zip Code: —	Construction	Kimberly Kowalski	Jack hammer + wiring	Month 6 Year 93	$6 an hr Per Week	Month 4 Year 94	$6.25 Per Week	Company went broke. Boss always picked on me.
NOTE: State reason for and length of inactivity between present application date and last employer.								
Name: Central Hospital / Tel. No. — / Address: Washington St. / City: Scranton State: PA Zip Code: —	Mental hospital	Lynn Donovan	Clean up	Month ? Year —	$5.50 an hr Per Week	Month ? Year	same Per Week	I got better + was discharged.
NOTE: State reason for and length of inactivity between present application date and last employer.								

I certify that the information in this application is correct to the best of my knowledge and understand that any misstatement or omission of information is grounds for dismissal in accordance with Brown's policy. I authorize the references listed above to give you any and all information concerning my previous employment and any pertinent information they may have, personal or otherwise, and release all parties from all liability for any damage that may result from furnishing same to you. In consideration of my employment, I agree to conform to the rules and regulations of Brown's, and my employment and compensation can be terminated with or without cause, and with or without notice, at any time, at the option of either the Company or myself. I understand that no unit manager or representative of Brown's other than the President or Vice-President of the company, has any authority to enter into any agreement for employment for any specified period of time, or to make any agreement contrary to the foregoing. In some states, the law requires that Brown's have my written permission before obtaining consumer reports on me, and I hereby authorize Brown's to obtain such reports.

Applicant's Signature: _Smith, Albert C._

NOT TO BE FILLED OUT BY APPLICANT

(Store will enter dates as required.)

				Mailed	Completed
Tested		REFERENCE REQUESTS		not yet	
Physical examination scheduled for — I didn't get one.		CONSUMER REPORT			
Physical examination form completed		With Tax (W-4)			
		State With Tax			

Date of Emp.		
Dept or Div.	Regular / Part-time	
Job Title	Job Grade	
Job Code		
Compensation Arrangement: Make me an offer	Review Card prepared	Minor's Work Permit
Manager Approving	Timecard prepared	Proof of Birth
Employee No.	Rack No.	Training Material Given to Employee

Unit Name and Number: Albert Smith

INTERVIEWER'S COMMENTS: I really need a job now.

Prospect for
1.
2.

Albert C. Smith's Improved Application

Albert C. Smith's application has many mistakes. How many did you find? It would not make a good impression on any employer. It is messy, includes negative information, and has many other problems.

The example on the next two pages shows what Albert C. Smith's application might look like when properly filled out.

Look it over and see how many errors you found that were corrected on the improved version.

APPLICATION FOR EMPLOYMENT

PLEASE PRINT INFORMATION REQUESTED IN INK.

Date _April 1, 2000_

BROWN'S IS AN EQUAL OPPORTUNITY EMPLOYER and fully subscribes to the principles of Equal Employment Opportunity. Brown's has adopted an Affirmative Action Program to ensure that all applicants and employees are considered for hire, promotion, job status, without regard to race, color, religion, sex, national origin, age, handicap, or status as a disabled veteran or veteran of the Vietnam Era.

To protect the interests of all concerned, applicants for certain job assignments must pass a physical examination before they are hired.

Note: This application will be considered active for 90 days. If you have not been employed within this period and are still interested in employment at Brown's, please contact the office where you applied and request that your application be reactivated.

Name _Smith_ _Albert_ _Claude_ Social Security Number _411-76-2614_
Last / First / Middle (Please present your Social Security Card for review)

Address _1526 North Otter Street_ _Scranton_ _PA_ _18602_
Number / Street / City / State / Zip Code

County _____ Current phone or nearest phone _555-1212_

Previous Address _____ Best time of day to contact _after 12 p.m._
Number / Street / City / State / Zip Code

(Answer only if position for which you are applying requires driving)

If hired, can you furnish proof of age? ✔ Yes ___ No Licensed to drive car? ✔ Yes ___ No

If hired, can you furnish proof that you are legally entitled to work in U.S. ✔ Yes ___ No Is license valid in this state? ✔ Yes ___ No

Have you ever been employed by Brown's. Yes ___ No ✔ If so, when ___ Position ___

Have you a relative in the employment of Brown's Department Store? Yes ___ No ✔

A PHYSICAL OR MENTAL DISABILITY WILL NOT CAUSE REJECTION IF IN BROWN'S MEDICAL OPINION YOU ARE ABLE TO SATISFACTORILY PERFORM IN THE POSITION FOR WHICH YOU ARE BEING CONSIDERED. Alternative placement, if available, of an applicant who does not meet the physical standards of the job for which he/she was originally considered is permitted.

Do you have any physical or mental impairment which may limit your ability to perform the job for which you are applying? _No_

If yes, what can reasonably be done to accommodate your limitation? ___

	School Attended	No. of Years	Name of School	City/State	Graduate?	Course or College Major	Average Grades
EDUCATION	Grammar	6	Holy Trinity	Scranton, PA		General	B
	Jr. High	3	Crestview Junior H.S.	Scranton, PA		General	B
	Sr. High	3	Warren Central H.S.	Scranton, PA		College Prep	C
	Other	—			—		—
	College	3	Indiana-Purdue University at Indpls	Indpls, IN		Electronics in progress	B

	Branch of Service	Date Entered Service	Date of Discharge	Highest Rank Held	Service-Related Skills and Experience Applicable to Civilian Employment
MILITARY SERVICE	United States Air Force	6-2-94	4-15-98	A/1C Airman First Class	Radio and small electronics repair

What experience or training have you had other than your work experience, military service and education? (Community activities, hobbies, etc.) ___

I am interested in the type of work I have checked:

Sales ✔ Office ___ Mechanical ___ Warehouse ___ Other (Specify): _Repair_

Or the following specific job ___

I am seeking (check only one):
___ Temporary employment (6 days or less)
___ Seasonal employment (one season, e.g. Christmas)
✔ Regular employment (employment for indefinite period of time)

I am available for (check only one)
___ Part-Time
✔ Full-Time Work

If part-time, indicate maximum hours per week and enter hours available in block to the right.

If temporary, indicate dates available ___

Have you been convicted during the past seven years of a serious crime involving a person's life or property?

NO ✔ YES ___ If yes, explain: ___

HOURS AVAILABLE FOR WORK		
Sunday	8 a.m.	To close
Monday	8 a.m.	To close
Tuesday	8 a.m.	To close
Wednesday	8 a.m.	To close
Thursday	8 a.m.	To close
Friday	8 a.m.	To close
Saturday	8 a.m.	To close

REFERENCES

LIST BELOW YOUR FOUR MOST RECENT EMPLOYERS, BEGINNING WITH THE CURRENT OR MOST RECENT ONE. IF YOU HAVE HAD FEWER THAN FOUR EMPLOYERS, USE THE REMAINING SPACES FOR PERSONAL REFERENCES. IF YOU WERE EMPLOYED UNDER A MAIDEN OR OTHER NAME, PLEASE ENTER THAT NAME IN THE RIGHT HAND MARGIN. IF APPLICABLE, ENTER SERVICE IN THE ARMED FORCES ON THE REVERSE SIDE.

NAMES AND ADDRESSES OF FORMER EMPLOYERS BEGINNING WITH THE CURRENT OR MOST RECENT	Nature of Employer's Business	Name of Your Supervisor	What kind of work did you do?	Starting Date	Starting Pay	Date of Leaving	Pay at Leaving	Why did you leave? Give details
Name Fred Willis / Address 1275 E. 11th St. Tel. No. 555-2111 / City Scranton State PA Zip Code 18515	Electrical subcontractor	Rafael Castillo	Electrician helper	Month 8 Year 99	$280 Per Week	Month Present Year	$280 Per Week	Work slowdown — limited work schedule
NOTE: State reason for and length of inactivity between present application date and last employer. Did odd/independent jobs, college courses — 5 months								
Name Scranton Public Schools / Address 593 Walnut Ave. Tel. No 555-3111 / City Scranton State PA Zip Code 18505	Maintenance of school	Eric Burgess	Custodian	Month 7 Year 98	$260 Per Week	Month 3 Year 99	$260 Per Week	Desired a more demanding position
NOTE: State reason for and length of inactivity between present application date and last employer.								
Name Grand Forks Air Force Base-USAF / Address Hwy 2 Tel. No. 701-597-2112 / City Grand Forks State ND Zip Code 58211	U.S. Air Force	Technical Sergeant Denise Hager	Small electronics + radio repair	Month 1 Year 95	$250 Per Week	Month 4 Year 98	$275 Per Week	Term of service expired — Honorable Discharge
NOTE: State reason for and length of inactivity between present application date and last employer. Completed basic training + electronics repair school — 6 mos.								
Name Wayne Construction / Address 1436 N. Anderson Dr. Tel. No. 555-4141 / City Scranton State PA Zip Code 18509	Heavy + light constr.	Kim Lenski	Electronic equipment installer	Month 6 Year 93	$240 Per Week	Month 4 Year 94	$250 Per Week	Company went out of business — joined U.S. Air Force

I certify that the information in this application is correct to the best of my knowledge and understand that any misstatement or omission of information is grounds for dismissal in accordance with Brown's policy. I authorize the references listed above to give you any and all information concerning my previous employment and any pertinent information they may have, personal or otherwise, and release all parties from all liability for any damage that may result from furnishing same to you. In consideration of my employment, I agree to conform to the rules and regulations of Brown's, and my employment and compensation can be terminated with or without cause, and with or without notice, at any time, at the option of either the Company or myself. I understand that no unit manager or representative of Brown's other than the President or Vice-President of the company, has any authority to enter into any agreement for employment for any specified period of time, or to make any agreement contrary to the foregoing. In some states, the law requires that Brown's have my written permission before obtaining consumer reports on me, and I hereby authorize Brown's to obtain such reports.

Applicant's Signature _Albert C. Smith_

NOT TO BE FILLED OUT BY APPLICANT

(Store will enter dates as required.)

INTERVIEWER'S COMMENTS				REFERENCE REQUESTS	Mailed	Completed
	Date of Emp.		Tested			
	Dept or Div.	Regular / Part-time	Physical examination scheduled for	CONSUMER REPORT		
	Job Title Code	Job Grade	Physical examination form completed	With. Tax (W-4)		
	Compensation Arrangement			State With. Tax		
	Manager Approving		Review Card prepared	Minor's Work Permit		
	Employee No.	Rack No.	Timecard prepared	Proof of Birth		
Prospect for 1. 2.				Training Material Given to Employee		

Unit Name and Number _____

PREPARATION: THE KEY TO SUCCESSFUL APPLICATIONS

Gary had the skills to do the job. That was not his problem. His problem was that he was not ready to fill out the application. He didn't have the information he needed. He felt confused and frustrated as a result.

You don't have to have the same experience. You can prepare yourself to do a good job on applications. You can make an application work for you instead of against you if you do the following:

- Learn what to expect from most applications.

- Present the best possible impression.

- Gather the needed information in advance.

SYSTEM-PROMPTED APPLICATIONS

Some companies have a new way to fill out job applications. These *system-prompted* applications are filled out on a computer at the employer's office or on the Internet. Even though it might sound complicated, don't let a computer-based application scare you. You should still fill it out the same way you would fill out a paper application.

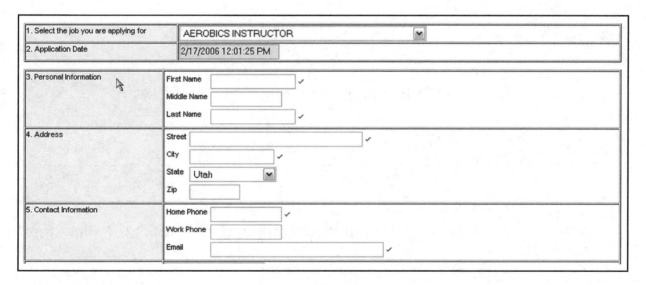

As you can see from the picture above, the information and questions on a system-prompted application are very similar to those on a paper application. If you have to fill out an application on a computer, don't be nervous. Just remember the following rules:

- Neatness still counts.

- Make sure your spelling, grammar, and capitalization are correct.

- It's still important to have the details you need, such as addresses and phone numbers, with you as you complete an electronic application.

- If you are completing the electronic application at the employer's location, feel free to ask the staff there how to use the system. If you are completing an application on the Internet, make sure you have all the information you need before you complete the process.

- Take your time and be relaxed.

System-prompted applications are just a more efficient way for employers to gather information about you. Don't be afraid of them. You can use the same methods you learn in Part 3 to complete them.

 checkpoint

Answer the questions that follow to review what you have learned in this chapter.

1. Why do employers use application forms?

_____

_____

_____

2. What are four qualities that employers look for in job seekers?

_____

_____

_____

3. Why did Gary have trouble with the job application form at the shoe store?

_____

_____

_____

4. What does it mean to be "screened out"?

_____

_____

_____

 challenge: Describe Your Qualities

Think of a job you might apply for. Then look at the four qualities listed below that employers want in their workers. In the spaces provided, write about how you can show an employer that you have these qualities.

1. I can do the job because...

_____

_____

_____

2. I am reliable because...

_____

_____

_____

3. I can be trusted because...

_____

_____

_____

4. I will work hard because...

_____

_____

_____

chapter 13

Gather Information for Your Application

THE GOALS OF THIS CHAPTER ARE

- To use more powerful words on your application

- To understand and be able to complete each major section of an application form

- To develop an inventory of information to use in answering any question on your application

GATHERING THE FACTS

In Chapter 12, you learned how employers use applications to help screen people in or out. You also received some general information about how to complete and use an application.

Now you will begin to work with actual applications. This chapter has worksheets to help you gather the facts you will need to fill out your applications. When you are through completing the worksheets, make copies to take with you when you fill out a "real" application and apply for a job.

THE POWER OF WORDS

The words you use on your application are important. Study the list of action words on the following worksheet. Using these words to describe your work experience can make it more positive. These words can help you make a good impression.

Use these or other action words as you fill out the other worksheets in this chapter. Action words are very good to use to describe your skills and accomplishments. Action words like these give an employer a very positive impression. They help you tell an employer what you can do.

Action words are important tools to use during your job search. You can use these words on applications. You can also use them in your interviews.

Action Words for Applications and Interviews

Look over the list of action words. You probably do many of these tasks or use many of these skills. In your mind, do a quick review of your work experience, education, and life experience. Then place a check in front of every word in the list that you can use to describe your experience on your applications.

This exercise will help you use the power of words to your benefit. Feel free to add your own action words to the list. Then use these and other action words in the worksheets and sample applications throughout this book.

❏ accept	❏ acquire	❏ allocate	❏ analyze
❏ anticipate	❏ approve	❏ arrange	❏ assemble
❏ assist	❏ assume	❏ authorize	❏ change
❏ compare	❏ consider	❏ contact	❏ contribute
❏ control	❏ coordinate	❏ counsel	❏ create
❏ decide	❏ define	❏ demonstrate	❏ design
❏ determine	❏ develop	❏ direct	❏ encourage
❏ evaluate	❏ execute	❏ exercise	❏ furnish
❏ give	❏ guide	❏ handle	❏ identify
❏ improve	❏ maintain	❏ make	❏ manage
❏ meet	❏ monitor	❏ organize	❏ plan
❏ prepare	❏ procure	❏ progress	❏ promote
❏ purchase	❏ receive	❏ recommend	❏ report
❏ require	❏ resources	❏ review	❏ schedule
❏ secure	❏ select	❏ ship	❏ stimulate
❏ strengthen	❏ supervise	❏ supply	❏ teach
❏ test	❏ train	❏ upgrade	❏ utilize

(continued)

(continued)

List your additional action words here:

_____   _____   _____

_____   _____   _____

_____   _____   _____

DEAL WITH NEGATIVE INFORMATION

The worksheets that follow will ask you for some information that many applications will not ask. Keep in mind that an application is often used to screen you out. If you give negative details about yourself, it will not help you.

Some questions in the worksheets are designed to get information that could get you screened out. The worksheet tips will give you ideas on how to answer these questions in a positive way.

"Illegal" Questions

Laws have been passed to keep employers from using certain information to make a decision about hiring. For this reason, most applications do not ask for information about age, race, religion, national origin, disabilities, or other personal details.

We, however, may ask the information here only to help you plan. For example, do you have a reliable way to get to work? If you have children, have you arranged for good child care? These questions may not be asked on an application, but you need to consider them. These things may come up in an interview. Thinking about them here will help you answer those concerns, even if the employer does not ask.

You may also find that some applications will ask for this information. In some cases, this information is allowed in order to make hiring decisions about certain jobs or to ensure that job requirements are met. For example, a firefighter would be required to lift heavy weight (to save an unconscious person) and climb ladders.

In other cases, the employer may be using out-of-date applications that ask questions that are no longer legal. That is another reason we have included some of these items on the worksheets. These items will have an asterisk (*) in front of them.

Telling the Truth

If you feel that answering a question will hurt you, the best thing to do may be to leave that question blank. This is often better than giving details that will get you screened out. Later, during an interview or after you get a job offer, you may tell the employer what you left off the application. But never lie on an application since that can result in your being fired later.

> ### FOCUS
>
> *If you feel that answering a question will hurt you, leave that question blank.*

YOUR APPLICATION INVENTORY

The word "inventory" refers to an organized collection of information. In this chapter, you will put together an inventory of your own. You will use this inventory to keep and organize the information you need to fill out applications. Later you can use it to complete an actual job application.

There are many types of application forms. Some are short and simple. Others are long and more complex. Most applications need the same type of information, but there can be differences. The inventory you will create in this chapter is very complete. It will help you fill out almost any application.

The worksheets that follow will help you build your inventory. Completing each worksheet will help you fill out a section of an application. For example, the personal information worksheet will help you gather the facts about yourself that many applications need. There are other worksheets for work history, education, and other sections of an application.

Each worksheet has tips to help you gather information or complete an application. Remember, items with an asterisk (*) may be illegal to ask on a real application form.

NEATNESS COUNTS

- The neater and more thoroughly you fill out each worksheet, the better you will do on your applications.

- Make sure each and every entry is as accurate as it can be.

- Use a pencil or erasable pen on all the worksheets so that you can make changes if necessary.

Inventory Section I
Personal Information

This worksheet collects personal information about you. Complete each entry as well as you can. Make sure your facts are correct and accurate.

Last name: _____

First name: _____ Middle name: _____

Street address: _____

_____

City: _____ State/province: _____ ZIP code: _____

> *Tip:* Include details such as an apartment number on the second address line.

Phone number: _____
OPTIONAL

Phone number for messages: _____

E-mail/Internet address: _____

Cell phone or pager numbers: _____

_____

Other ways to reach you: _____

_____

> *Tip:* Include your area code with all phone numbers. If you do not have a phone or answering machine, ask a friend or relative if employers can leave a message there. You may need to write down more than one number if your phone is not answered during the daytime. That is when most employers will call. Just be sure you make it easy for a potential employer to reach you! Finally, if you have a cell phone, pager, e-mail address, or other ways to be contacted, write these down as well.

*How long have you lived at your present address?

Years: _____ Months: _____

Previous street address: _____

City:_____ State/province: _____ ZIP code: _____

*How long have you lived there? _____

> *Tip:* Few applications will ask the question above, but some might. If you have moved many times, you may want to write down several addresses on this worksheet.

*Social Security number (or SSN):_____

> *Tip:* You should have a Social Security card with your name and number on it. This is a nine-digit number assigned to citizens of the United States. It is used by employers to keep track of the taxes and other deductions they send to the government. Everyone gets a Social Security number. You can get your own number at any age. If you do not have a Social Security card, contact your local Social Security Administration office for details. You can find its phone number and address in the blue pages of your regular phone directory. Look under "U.S. Government, Social Security Administration." You can also get information from Social Security's Web site at http://www.ssa.gov.

Are you a citizen of the United States?_____

> *Tip:* Many employers are now required to ask for proof that you are a citizen of this country. If you are not, you may be required to show legal papers that allow you to live and work in this country. Employers can be fined for hiring workers who are not legal citizens.

Position you are applying for:_____

> *Tip:* Many applications say "Position Desired?" This means the same thing as the statement above. When you fill out an actual application, you may know of a job opening there that interests you. If so, write that job title in the space. If not, write down a general title, such as "Office Worker." If you are too specific, the employer may screen you out even if another job is open in your general area. Whatever you put down, don't say you'll do just anything.

Schedule of hours desired:_____ a.m./p.m. to _____ a.m./p.m.

(continued)

(continued)

Can you work nights?_____What hours?_____

Can you work weekends?_____What hours?_____

> *Tip:* Before you fill out an application, have a clear idea of what hours you can work. For example:

- Do you want to work full time or part time?

- Do you want a flexible schedule (that changes from week to week) or do you want to always work the same hours?

- Are you willing to work nights and weekends or only daytime hours during the week?

- Can you sometimes work extra hours?

Most people want to work weekdays. If you are willing to work nights or weekends, you may get a job over someone who is not. Many employers will also need you to work some overtime. The more flexible you are, the more likely you are to get some jobs.

*How will you get to work? What is your backup plan, in case your regular transportation fails?

_____

_____

_____

_____

> *Tip:* You may not be asked how you will get to work. Some employers just want to know that you can get to work every day on time. Think about how you will get to work. Will you be able to get to work every day, on time? Your answers must convince the employer that you will not miss work due to transportation problems.

Pay or salary desired:_____

> *Tip:* This can be a tricky question. An employer wants to know if you are expecting more money than the job pays. If you write the wrong thing here, an employer may eliminate you right away. Don't write a dollar amount if you can avoid it. It is better to write "open" or "negotiable"

instead. This way, an employer will not screen you out based on what you write.

Find out how much this type of job pays in your area. Later, in the interview, you can mention a pay range such as "seven to nine dollars an hour" or the "mid 20s" if the employer asks. That way you won't be eliminated from a job you may want.

*Date of birth:_____

> *Tip:* It is illegal to discriminate based on age. For this reason, most applications will not ask the question above. Child labor laws limit the number of hours and the type of work teenagers are allowed to do, and some jobs require you to be 21 years old. Employers can ask your age to make sure they are not breaking a law by hiring you.

The application may ask if you are over 16 or 21 years of age. If the job requires workers over a certain age, you may be asked to show proof of age.

*Sex (or gender): _____ *Height: _____ *Weight: _____

*Marital status: _____

> *Tip:* The preceding questions are not often asked on an application. Like other illegal questions, you are not required to answer them unless the job requires it. If you are afraid your answers might work against you (screen you out), consider leaving them blank.

*How many dependents do you have? _____

> *Tip:* Dependents are children or other people, including yourself, who depend on you to support them. You claim dependents when you file your tax returns. An employer will need to know this for tax purposes. It is not information often needed on an application before you are hired, and you could leave this item blank. You can also write down "1" if you are claiming only yourself. If you are married, write "2" and continue to add for each child.

*Have you ever been bonded (*or* can you be bonded?): _____

> *Tip:* Some employers buy a special insurance for staff who handle money, go into customers' homes, or other situations. The insurance covers any loss

(continued)

(continued)

to the employer due to theft and certain other situations. If you had ever been bonded, you would know it. Often, the insurance company will check your arrest record before insuring you.

*Have you ever been arrested? If yes, give details:

_____

_____

_____

_____

> *Tip:* It is legal to ask if you have ever been *convicted* of a felony (a major crime). In this country, being arrested is not the same as being guilty. Arrests for minor crimes (misdemeanors) do not have to be mentioned at all. Arrests or convictions while you were a juvenile are kept confidential and also do not need to be mentioned. For this reason, few applications will ask if you have been arrested. Some will ask if you have been convicted of a felony. If you have not been, say "No." If you have, it may be wise to leave the question blank and bring it up only if you get offered the job.

*Do you have any physical or emotional limitations in doing the job you are applying for? If yes, please describe:

_____

_____

_____

_____

> *Tip:* If you can do the job, an employer is not allowed to discriminate based on a disability. A disability matters only if it prevents you from doing the work required by that particular job. In most cases, your answer should be "No" or "None that would interfere with my ability to perform the job."

If you have a disability, you should not consider a job that you cannot do. For example, you may not be able to lift over 20 pounds. Or maybe you get dizzy if you climb a ladder. If so, you should not apply for a job that requires heavy lifting or working at heights where you are not comfortable. As long as you avoid these types of jobs, your limitation or disability is not a problem.

*Have you had any serious illness or injury in the past five years? If yes, please describe:

_____

_____

_____

_____

Tip: Unless you missed more than two weeks of work from an illness or injury, write "No." An application may also ask if you have ever made a worker's compensation claim. An employer wants to know because this will increase insurance costs. A past illness or injury may also limit your ability to do the job. Or you might miss more work than average if you get ill again. But employers are not allowed to discriminate against you because of past injury or illness, so you can often leave the above item blank.

Do you have a valid driver's license? Have you received any speeding or other traffic citations over the past three years?   ❑ Yes   ❑ No

If yes, please explain:

_____

_____

_____

_____

Tip: Most applications will not ask these questions unless you are expected to drive as part of the job. You need to list major violations only, not parking tickets and minor violations. Include any information you can to explain a major ticket. If the job does not require you to drive, you can leave the above item blank.

think about it

Now it's time to fill out the personal information section of a sample application. Few real applications will be as complete, and this one includes information not covered in the worksheet.

Remember to follow directions carefully. Employers need to know that you can pay attention and follow directions on the job. So if you are asked to print on the application, be sure to *print* rather than write. If it asks you to list your last name, then your first name, do it the way it asks. Pay attention to directions!

Notice to Applicants: Please print your responses neatly to all questions.

APPLICATION FOR EMPLOYMENT

PERSONAL DATA

Name _____ Social Security No. _____

Present Address _____

Telephone Number _____ How Long Have You Lived at Present Address? _____

Previous Address _____ How Long? _____

Position Applied for: _____ Work Schedule Desired: ☐ Full-Time ☐ Part-Time

   If Part-Time, Specify Hours Desired by Day: Sun. _____

   Mon. _____ Wed. _____ Fri. _____

   Tues. _____ Thurs. _____ Sat. _____

Rate of pay expected: Start _____ 6 Mo. _____ 1 Year _____

How did you hear of this opening? _____

_____

Have you worked with us before? ☐ No ☐ Yes—When/How Long? _____

Previous Job Title _____ Reason for Leaving _____

List any friends/relatives working with us now _____

List any special skills you have for position applied for above _____

Are you over 21? ☐ Yes ☐ No (If No, hire is subject to minimum legal age verification.)

Sex: ☐ Male ☐ Female Height: _____ Ft. _____ In. Weight _____ lbs.

Marital Status: ☐ Single ☐ Married ☐ Separated ☐ Divorced ☐ Widowed

No. Years Married _____ No. of Dependents _____

Have you ever been bonded? ☐ No ☐ Yes—When? _____

Have you ever been convicted of a crime in the past 10 years? (Excluding traffic violations)

   ☐ No ☐ Yes—If Yes, describe convictions _____

Do you have any physical handicaps preventing you from doing certain types of work?

   ☐ No ☐ Yes—If Yes, describe handicap/limitations _____

Have you had any serious illness in the past 5 years? ☐ No ☐ Yes—If Yes, describe _____

_____

_____

_____

Inventory Section II
Employment Information

Use the next worksheet to gather information about jobs you've had before.

On an actual application, you will usually be asked to list jobs starting with the most recent one. Do the same with this worksheet. Include nonpaid work as well, such as volunteer positions you have had.

Use blank sheets of paper if you have had more work experience than you can fit on this worksheet.

Job 1 (Your Most Recent Job)

Employer's name:_____

Employer's street address: _____

City:_____ State/province: _____ ZIP code: _____

Position/job title:_____

Starting date:_____ Ending date:_____

Beginning salary:_____ Ending salary:_____

Responsibilities:

_____

_____

_____

_____

Tip: Use the above section to list everything you did on a job. Include skills, accomplishments, results, equipment used, new skills you learned, training you received, people you trained or supervised, and other details. Be sure to include all the positive things you did.

Tools or equipment you used: _____

_____

_____

Tip: List any special tools or equipment that you used or learned how to use on this job.

Skills you learned or used:

_____

_____

Accomplishments, pay increases, and other positive details:

_____

_____

Reason for leaving:

_____

_____

Tip: State the truth, but put it in a positive way. Don't say "The boss was a jerk" or "got fired." It's better to say, "Needed a career change" or "they cut staff with less seniority."

Can we contact this employer? _____

Tip: Be ready for the above question. It may come up. If you had a supervisor who is not likely to give you a good recommendation, use the name of someone at that organization who will. The higher that person's position, the better.

Tip: If you provide the previous employer's address and telephone number, the potential employer might contact that organization with or without your agreement. If you know that someone won't speak highly of you, direct the new employer to the best possible person to talk to.

Supervisor's name: _____

Phone number: _____

E-mail address: _____

(continued)

(continued)

Job 2 (Your Next Most Recent Job)

Employer's name: _____

Employer's street address: _____

City:_____ State/province: _____ ZIP code: _____

Position/job title:_____

Starting date:_____ Ending date:_____

Beginning salary:_____ Ending salary:_____

Responsibilities:

_____

_____

_____

Tools or equipment you used:

_____

_____

Skills you learned or used:

_____

_____

Accomplishments, pay increases, and other positive details:

_____

_____

Reason for leaving:

_____

_____

Can we contact this employer?_____

Supervisor's name: _____

Phone number: _____ E-mail address:_____

Job 3 (Your Next Most Recent Job)

Employer's name: _____

Employer's street address: _____

City:_____ State/province: _____ ZIP code: _____

Position/job title:_____

Starting date:_____ Ending date:_____

Beginning salary:_____ Ending salary:_____
Responsibilities:

_____

_____

_____

Tools or equipment you used:

_____

_____

Skills you learned or used:

_____

_____

Accomplishments, pay increases, and other positive details:

_____

_____

_____

(continued)

(continued)

Reason for leaving:

_____

_____

Can we contact this employer?_____

Supervisor's name: _____

Phone number: _____ E-mail address:_____

 think about it

Use the sample portion of an application to practice filling out your previous employment information.

Be as complete as you can.

EMPLOYMENT

Please give accurate, complete full-time and part-time employment record. Start with present or most recent employer.

1

Company Name	Telephone ( )
Address	Employed (State Month and Year) From: To:
Name of Supervisor	Weekly Pay Start: Last:
State Job Title and Describe Your Work	Reason for Leaving

2

Company Name	Telephone ( )
Address	Employed (State Month and Year) From: To:
Name of Supervisor	Weekly Pay Start: Last:
State Job Title and Describe Your Work	Reason for Leaving

3

Company Name	Telephone ( )
Address	Employed (State Month and Year) From: To:
Name of Supervisor	Weekly Pay Start: Last:
State Job Title and Describe Your Work	Reason for Leaving

4

Company Name	Telephone ( )
Address	Employed (State Month and Year) From: To:
Name of Supervisor	Weekly Pay Start: Last:
State Job Title and Describe Your Work	Reason for Leaving

5

Company Name	Telephone ( )
Address	Employed (State Month and Year) From: To:
Name of Supervisor	Weekly Pay Start: Last:
State Job Title and Describe Your Work	Reason for Leaving

We may contact the employers listed above unless you indicate those you do not want us to contact.

DO NOT CONTACT

Employer Number(s) _____ Reason _____

Inventory Section III
Education and Training Information

Your education and training can be very important to an employer. This worksheet will help you collect the details. It includes sections for all the schools you have attended. It also has sections for training. This would include any formal training as well as training you received at home, in a family business, or other places. Be sure to look over this worksheet before you begin writing.

Elementary School

Name of school: _____

Street address: _____

City:_____ State/province: _____ ZIP code: _____

Last grade completed: _____Did you graduate? _____

Junior High/Middle School

Name of school: _____

Street address: _____

City:_____ State/province: _____ ZIP code: _____

Last grade completed: _____Did you graduate? _____

Special skills, training, and honors. List any special skills, training, awards, activities, clubs, or organizations from your junior high school years that might interest an employer:

_____

_____

High School

Name of school: _____

Street address: _____

City:_____ State/province: _____ ZIP code: _____

Last grade completed: _____Did you graduate? _____

> *Tip:* If you didn't receive a diploma from the high school you attended, but
> you have received your GED (General Equivalency Diploma), answer
> "Yes" to the above question.

Grade point average (GPA): _____

Courses: _____

_____

_____

> *Tip:* List any courses you took that relate to the job you want.

Special skills, training, and honors. List any special skills, training, awards, activities, clubs, or organizations from your high school years that might interest an employer:

_____

_____

_____

_____

College, Trade, or Technical School

Name of school: _____

Street address: _____

City:_____ State/province: _____ ZIP code: _____

Last grade completed: _____Did you graduate? _____

Degree or certificate: _____

Grade point average (GPA): _____

Courses: _____

(continued)

(continued)

> *Tip:* List any courses you took that relate to the job you want.
>
> Special skills, training, and honors. List any special skills, training, awards, activities, clubs, or organizations from your post high school years that might interest an employer:
>
> _____
>
> _____
>
> _____
>
> _____
>
> ### Other Training or Education
>
> _____
>
> _____

 think about it

List any other training or education you have received. This might include workshops, seminars, formal training on a job, or military training. Also include things you learned informally. For example, you might have worked summers on your Uncle Ed's farm. There you learned to work on farm equipment and to take care of animals.

Think about what you know how to do. You should include it here even if you didn't learn it in school. Don't miss the opportunity to show off your special skills and knowledge!

_____

_____

_____

_____

think about it

Fill out the education and training section of the sample portion of an application.

It is more complete than most applications, so it will give you some good practice that will help you when you fill out a real application.

	School	Name and Location of School	Course of Study	No. of Years Completed	Did You Graduate?	Degree or Diploma
EDUCATION	College				☐ YES ☐ NO	
	High				☐ YES ☐ NO	
	Elementary				☐ YES ☐ NO	
	Other				☐ YES ☐ NO	

AWARDS AND HONORS
(List special certificates, awards, and honors below)

Inventory Section IV
Military Service Information

Complete this section if you have been in the military. This experience can be as important as any other work experience you've had.

Branch: _____ Rank: _____

Years of service: _____From: _____To: _____

Duties:

_____

_____

_____

In the spaces below, list any special duties or responsibilities you had to help describe the type of job or position you held.

_____

_____

_____

_____

Salary: _____

Details of any promotions: _____

_____

_____

Explain in the spaces below any special circumstances of a promotion. For example, perhaps you had outstanding job performances, a superior rating, or took part in a successful training exercise.

_____

_____

_____

_____

Special skills, training, and awards. List any special education such as schools or courses you attended, training, or skills you acquired during your military service. Be sure to list any awards such as ribbons and medals:

_____

_____

_____

_____

 think about it

Use the sample portion of an application to practice filling out your military service information.

Leave the sheet blank if you have not been in the military.

	BRANCH	ENLISTMENT RANK	HIGHEST RANK HELD	SALARY		REASON FOR CHANGE IN RANK
				FROM	TO	
MILITARY						

DESCRIBE DUTIES:

SCHOOLS OR COURSES ATTENDED	LENGTH		DID YOU GRADUATE?	CERTIFICATE OR DIPLOMA
	WEEKS	MONTHS		
1.			☐ YES ☐ NO	
2.			☐ YES ☐ NO	
3.			☐ YES ☐ NO	
4.			☐ YES ☐ NO	

LIST ANY SPECIAL SKILLS ACQUIRED DURING YOUR MILITARY SERVICE:

WHAT IS A REFERENCE?

A reference is a person an employer can contact to find out more about you. For example, many employers will want to contact your previous employers. They do this to find out if you are a good worker. Other people who know you well can also be used as a reference. This might include teachers, coaches, or others who know you.

Before listing someone as a reference, be sure that he or she will say good things about you. The best people to use are those who know that you are a good worker and can be depended on to do a good job. This includes former employers and co-workers.

Former teachers or coaches might make good references. Supervisors from volunteer positions are also helpful. An application for a job might request references both from previous jobs and from personal experiences.

Contact people you know and ask their permission to use them as references. Ask what they will say about you. It will help to tell them what kind of job you are looking for and the skills you have to do that job. If you feel that they will say good things about you, get their correct mailing address and phone number.

As you talk to your references, ask whether they know about any job openings. They may know of someone who could use a person with your skills. Ask them to keep you in mind if they hear about a job that might interest you. This is called *networking,* and it's one of the most effective job search methods!

> ## FOCUS
>
> *Ask your references to keep you in mind if they hear about a job that might interest you.*

Inventory Section V
References Information

List the people you know from work experiences and from your personal life who will be able to talk about your skills and abilities that relate to the job you want. Include former school teachers or coaches. Also list people you know who will say good things about you or give you a good recommendation.

(continued)

(continued)

Work References

> *Tip:* If you don't have much formal work experience, include names of people who have paid you to do babysitting, lawn mowing, or other odd jobs. If you have done volunteer work, you can include the name of a supervisor who knows you from this.

Name of reference: _____

Relationship (How does this person know you?): _____

Name of organization: _____

Street address: _____

City:_____ State/province: _____

ZIP code: _____ Phone number: _____

E-mail address: _____

What will this person say about you? _____

_____

_____

> *Tip:* It is good to write down something about yourself that this person could tell your next employer. This way, when you ask this person to be your reference, you can also provide him or her with something good to say. Many times this person will say these things as long as the information is true.

Did this person give you permission to be used as a reference? _____

Name of reference: _____

Relationship (How does this person know you?): _____

Name of organization: _____

Street address: _____

City:_____ State/province: _____

ZIP code: _____ Phone number: _____

E-mail address: _____

What will this person say about you? _____

_____

_____

Did this person give you permission to be used as a reference? _____

Name of reference: _____

Relationship (How does this person know you?): _____

Name of organization: _____

Street address: _____

City:_____ State/province: _____

ZIP code: _____ Phone number: _____

E-mail address: _____

What will this person say about you? _____

_____

_____

Did this person give you permission to be used as a reference? _____

College, Trade, or Technical School References

Tip: List any teacher or other staff, such as an advisor, who might serve as a good reference for you.

Name of reference: _____

Relationship (How does this person know you?): _____

Name of organization: _____

Street address: _____

City:_____ State/province: _____

(continued)

(continued)

ZIP code: _____ Phone number: _____

E-mail address: _____

What will this person say about you? _____

_____

_____

Did this person give you permission to be used as a reference? _____

Name of reference: _____

Relationship (How does this person know you?): _____

Name of organization: _____

Street address: _____

City:_____ State/province: _____

ZIP code: _____ Phone number: _____

E-mail address: _____

What will this person say about you? _____

_____

_____

Did this person give you permission to be used as a reference? _____

Name of reference: _____

Relationship (How does this person know you?): _____

Name of organization: _____

Street address: _____

City:_____ State/province: _____

ZIP code: _____ Phone number: _____

E-mail address: _____

What will this person say about you? _____
_____
_____

Did this person give you permission to be used as a reference? _____

High School References

Tip: List any teachers, coaches, or other staff from high school who would give you a good recommendation to an employer.

Name of reference: _____

Relationship (How does this person know you?): _____

Name of organization: _____

Street address: _____

City:_____ State/province: _____

ZIP code: _____ Phone number: _____

E-mail address: _____

What will this person say about you? _____
_____
_____

Did this person give you permission to be used as a reference? _____

Name of reference: _____

Relationship (How does this person know you?): _____

Name of organization: _____

Street address: _____

City:_____ State/province: _____

ZIP code: _____ Phone number: _____

(continued)

(continued)

E-mail address: _____

What will this person say about you? _____

_____

_____

Did this person give you permission to be used as a reference? _____

Name of reference: _____

Relationship (How does this person know you?): _____

Name of organization: _____

Street address: _____

City:_____ State/province: _____

ZIP code: _____ Phone number: _____

E-mail address: _____

What will this person say about you? _____

_____

_____

Did this person give you permission to be used as a reference? _____

Personal References

> *Tip:* Pick people who are not your relatives but who know you well. List people you know from local businesses or organizations, church or synagogue, or anyone else who has personal knowledge of your character.

Name of reference: _____

Relationship (How does this person know you?): _____

Name of organization: _____

Street address: _____

City:_____ State/province: _____

ZIP code: _____ Phone number: _____

E-mail address: _____

What will this person say about you? _____

_____

_____

Did this person give you permission to be used as a reference? _____

Name of reference: _____

Relationship (How does this person know you?): _____

Name of organization: _____

Street address: _____

City:_____ State/province: _____

ZIP code: _____ Phone number: _____

E-mail address: _____

What will this person say about you? _____

_____

_____

Did this person give you permission to be used as a reference? _____

Name of reference: _____

Relationship (How does this person know you?): _____

Name of organization: _____

Street address: _____

City:_____ State/province: _____

ZIP code: _____ Phone number: _____

(continued)

(continued)

E-mail address: _____

What will this person say about you? _____

_____

_____

Did this person give you permission to be used as a reference? _____

 think about it

Practice completing the references section. After you collect the data you need, complete the practice application section. Choose the best references from any category that you listed before. These should not be former employers or relatives. Later, you can use this information to help you complete real applications.

		NAME AND OCCUPATION	ADDRESS	PHONE NUMBER
REFERENCE CHECK	1.			
	2.			
	3.			

checkpoint

Answer the following questions to review what you have learned in this chapter.

1. Is your application inventory complete? Go back over the worksheets and look for any trouble spots. If you don't know how to find certain information, ask for help. Ask a friend, a librarian, a teacher, or someone else. The more complete your inventory, the more confidence you'll have when you do your real applications! List trouble spots or areas where you need to gather more information.

_____

_____

_____

_____

_____

2. Completing your application inventory can make you more aware of your special skills and strengths. With these in mind, what are some jobs that you might be suited for? List them below.

_____

_____

_____

_____

_____

challenge: Describe the Perfect Job

1. In the space that follows, describe your perfect job. What type of job would it be? What sorts of things would you do? How would you spend your time?

_____

_____

_____

_____

2. If you were to apply for that job today, would you be qualified? If not, what experience, training, or skills would you need so that you could get that job?

_____

_____

_____

_____

chapter 14

How to Use an Application in Your Job Search

THE GOALS OF THIS CHAPTER ARE

- To review the major points you have learned in Part 3 of this book

- To learn techniques for using the application in the job search

- To understand how an employer will use an application in the screening process

PUT IT ALL TOGETHER

In Chapter 12, you learned some basic information about applications. You learned what they are and how they are used. You also learned that applications are often used to screen you out. This makes it important to fill out an application in the right way.

In Chapter 13, you gathered information and put together your application inventory. This inventory now includes most of the information you need to fill out an application. You also practiced filling out sections of sample application forms. You learned how to use an application to make a good impression.

Now it's time to learn how to use the application in your job search. Let's begin by doing a quick review of the important points you've learned so far. Take the quiz that follows. It won't be graded, so just do your best.

Read each question and check whether you think the statement is true or false. When you are finished, read the "correct" answers to see how well you did.

Applications Review Quiz

Question	True	False
1. An application is one of the best tools you can use to get a job.	❑	❑
2. Employers use applications to look for reasons to hire you.	❑	❑
3. When filling out an application, you don't have to be completely honest.	❑	❑
4. Applications can help you get a job if you know how to do them well.	❑	❑
5. Applications can keep you from getting a job even if you are well qualified.	❑	❑

ANSWERS TO THE APPLICATIONS REVIEW QUIZ

1. **False.** Application forms don't make it easy for you to show off your best qualities. Many job search tools and methods are more effective. But since many employers use applications, learning to do applications well is an important part of your job search.

2. **False.** Employers actually use applications to look for reasons *not* to hire you. A quick glance at your application might make an employer think that you are any or all of the following:

   - too sloppy
   - underqualified
   - unreliable
   - overqualified

   These are just a few negative possibilities. Your task is to make a positive impression. Everyone has flaws. You need to convince an employer that your strengths make up for any weaknesses you might have.

3. **False.** Dishonesty is not a good idea in any part of your job search. An employer can fire you for lying on an application. It is better to leave a section blank if you think the information will hurt your chances of getting hired. You may want to save this information for the interview instead.

4. **True.** An application can help you get a job if it helps make a good first impression. Use it to present your strengths.

5. **True.** Employers often do not hire the best-qualified person. Why? Because these people don't always present themselves well. If your application makes a bad impression, you will be screened out right away.

MAKING APPLICATIONS WORK FOR YOU

You have already learned some tips on filling out each section of an application. In general, you can follow three rules in completing an application. Let's explore each one.

Rule 1: Be As Neat and Complete As Possible

We've covered some points under this rule already, but they are worth repeating. Neatness makes a positive impression. Messy applications make a negative one.

Neatness shows that you pay attention to details. It also shows that you are careful with your work, follow directions, and are willing to make the extra effort. These qualities mean a lot to an employer.

> ### FOCUS
> *Do not cross out mistakes. Use an erasable black ink pen.*

Print as neatly as you can. Do not cross out mistakes. Instead, use a black ink pen that erases. This will let you erase mistakes that you might make.

Read and follow all the directions carefully. Fill out each section completely and do not leave blank spaces if you can avoid it.

Rule 2: Be Positive

A positive attitude will serve you well in every part of your job search. Does being positive mean you should be less than honest? No. It means that you make sure that you include the positive things that you have done or can do. Even if something seems negative, try to include the positive side.

For example, suppose that you have had several jobs that show no clear direction. This could look negative to an employer. But what if you learned valuable skills on those jobs? Perhaps you learned to get along with many different people and situations. Or maybe you learned how to learn new skills quickly. Can employers appreciate qualities like these?

You bet they can! But you have to tell them about your skills. You have to make employers want to know more about you. That is, make them want to invite you to an interview.

Rule 3: Be Creative

It's hard to imagine being creative on an application form. It seems tough to force your life's experience into a bunch of boxes and lines. But you can do it. The trick is to use every space to your advantage.

Look at each space on an application form as an opportunity to present your skills and abilities. Avoid wasting words and make each word count. Use strong action words like the ones listed in Chapter 13. Include positive things about yourself, even if the form does not ask for this kind of information.

Think of how your skills and experiences support your present job objective. Make sure that you include these in your application. If you have something important to write but the box is too small or the lines stop, keep writing in blank space.

Just indicate how you are continuing the information—draw a small, neat arrow, for example, or write, "Please see back of form for more details."

EXAMPLE

Gary Tries Again

Do you remember Gary, who you read about in Chapter 12? Now you will find out what happened to him. Read his story below. After the story, you'll find a copy of an application that Gary filled out. Look at it for examples of how to be creative on your own job applications.

Networking Helps Gary Get Job Leads

Gary still needed a job. But he didn't want another experience like the one at the shoe store. He left there feeling confused and defeated.

Gary wondered whether selling shoes was really for him. He realized that he hadn't thought about that before he applied for the job.

Gary remembered the woman who had been filling out an application that same day. "I'm going to manage this store some day—or another one like it," she had said.

He thought of the way she had smiled when she said, "I know what I want." I know what I want. It was such a simple statement, but it made her seem so strong.

Gary knew he had a lot of thinking to do. But he was beginning to feel excited. This business of finding a job was more than just a way to pay the rent. It was a chance to figure out who he was, what he could be, and where he wanted his life to go. Maybe he wouldn't figure it out all at once. But that was okay. At least now he knew what to do. He needed to figure out what sort of job he really wanted.

There was no "Help Wanted" sign on the front door of Clark's Furniture Store. But Gary knew that the store might have a job opening. He'd been talking to everyone he knew, explaining that he was looking for work. Not just any work. He was looking for a job that required his best skills and knowledge. Gary told everyone he knew what skills he had and what kind of a job he wanted.

A friend of a friend of Gary's mentioned Clark's. The friend told him that Clark's had been growing. The store just might need someone to handle the increased business. Even though there might not be an opening now, Gary went to talk to the owner.

Gary's Application Turns into an Interview

Gary looked good—not too dressy for the place, but not too casual, either. He felt good. He had a notebook full of every kind of information he could possibly need for his application.

Gary went in the store and asked for Mr. Clark. They shook hands as Gary introduced himself. Gary explained that he was interested in working in the furniture business. He said that he was good with people, that he had some sales experience, and was not afraid of hard work. He also explained that he was willing to work evenings and weekends and asked Mr. Clark if he had time to speak about a job opening in his company.

Mr. Clark explained that he was busy now but gave Gary an application form to fill out. It was possible, Mr. Clark said, that he could use a person in the warehouse and that if Gary did well there, he could move into selling or other areas.

Gary took a seat and began carefully filling out the application. His notebook lay open beside him. When Gary was halfway through the application, a young woman came into the store. She wore blue jeans and sandals. "Do you have any job openings here?" Gary heard her ask a salesperson. The man gave her an application to fill out. "Do you have a pen?" the young woman asked.

(continued)

(continued)

> After a few minutes, she stopped writing. "Are you looking for a job too?" she asked Gary. He nodded and thought for a minute before he said, "I'm going to own a store like this some day." Then he smiled. "I know what I want," Gary said.
>
> After some time, Mr. Clark returned and looked over Gary's application. "Do you have a few minutes?" Mr. Clark asked. "Of course," Gary answered.
>
> "Let's go into my office and talk a little."
>
> Gary glanced behind him. The young woman was gone. She left her completed application on the table. Then Mr. Clark opened the door of his office, and Gary went in.

GARY'S COMPLETED APPLICATION

The facing page shows the application that Gary filled out. While this application could be improved, it is neat, complete, and mentions Gary's skills and accomplishments. Look it over carefully for ideas on filling out your own application.

HOW GARY GOT THE INTERVIEW

Gary got an interview by asking for it, not by filling out an application. Mr. Clark agreed to see him but also asked him to fill out an application. Gary's completed application helped make a good impression on Mr. Clark.

FOCUS

The one who gets the job is the one who gets the interview, not the one who completes the application.

Remember this in your own job search! Filling out applications might get you an interview, but it is also likely to get you screened out.

This is because many other job seekers will have more or better experience than you do. Or they have more education or training. If this is the case, you will probably be screened out on the basis of your application alone.

The one who gets the job is the one who gets the interview, not the one who completes the application. For this reason, it is important to always ask to see the person who would hire or supervise you. If that person asks you to fill out an application before he or she will talk to you, you will be well prepared.

Clark's Furniture

application for employment

PERSONAL INFORMATION

Date 8-28-99 S.S. No. 104-37-2729

Last Name Williams   First Gary   Middle M.   Age 25

Address 8293 Riverview Dr.   Height 5'11" Weight 175 Date of Birth 3-6-74

City Cleveland   State OH   Zip 72917

Telephone 219-464-3209

Status: Single ✓   Married ____ Widowed ____
Divorced ____ Separated ____

Have you ever worked for this company before? No   Location? ―   When? ―

FORMER EMPLOYERS   (List below last 3 employers, starting with the last one first)

Month & Year	Name and Address of Employer	Salary	Position	Reason for Leaving
From October 97	Mac's Machinery	Start $10 per hr	Warehouse worker	No upward mobility. No openings for me to move in to.
To Present	219 Stacie Lane, Euclid, OH Supervisor Mac Knife Ph:(219) 825-4317	Finish 18,000 yr.	Sales + delivery person	
Accomplishments	Promoted to counter sales because of the way I handle customers and solve their problems.			
From June 94	Marlin's Fresh Cannery	Start $8.50 hr	Dockworker	Industry slow-down forced Marlin's to go out of business.
To September 97	3171 Lakefront, Cleveland Supervisor Charlie Seashore Ph:(219) 823-7309	Finish $12.50 hr	Cannery worker	
Accomplishments	Because I was dependable and reliable, I moved into a position with more responsibility.			
From August 92	Yard Pro Lawn Service	Start $6.00 hr	Lawn care worker	I wanted full-time work, and this job was only seasonal and part-time
To April 94	411 Summer St., Cleveland Supervisor Brenda Green Ph:(219) 823-3490	Finish $7.50 hr	Lawn care worker	
Accomplishments	I worked at this job while I attended junior college and never missed a day of work or my classes.			

Have you ever been convicted of a Felony?   Yes ____   No ✓

In case of an emergency notify: June or Ed Williams   Phone: 219-464-2545

Citizen of U.S.A.? Yes ✓ No ____   If not, do you possess an alien registration card? ____

If yes, give registration card number:

EDUCATION

	Name & Location of School	Date Graduated	Subjects Studied
High School	Lake High School, 44 Boxelder Rd., Cleveland	1992	General Courses
College	Lakeport Junior College Rte. 3, Cleveland		Business
Other			

checkpoint

Answer the following questions to review what you have learned in this chapter.

1. What was different for Gary when he went to apply for a job this time?

_____

_____

_____

_____

_____

2. Do you think that the young woman who came in after Gary would be considered for the job? Explain your answer.

_____

_____

_____

_____

_____

3. Why is it important to have a job objective? (This question is important even if you are not actively involved in a job search at this time. Keeping your long-term goals in mind can get you through the tough times, such as training, or taking an entry-level job that's below the level you want to be.)

_____

_____

_____

_____

_____

challenge: Would You Hire Gary?

Look over Gary's application as if you were Mr. Clark of Clark's Furniture Store. See it through Mr. Clark's eyes. Would you hire Gary? Why or why not?

_____

_____

_____

_____

_____

chapter 15

Practice with Applications

THE GOALS OF THIS CHAPTER ARE

- To learn how to follow directions carefully when filling out applications

- To be able to present your "best" self on the application form

PUTTING PEN TO PAPER

This chapter includes three real application forms. You should fill out each one as if you were applying for a job. Each application form is different, but many ask for similar information.

Since many applications ask different questions, the samples here ask for information not included in earlier samples.

Read the directions carefully for each application and its sections *before* you fill it out. Also, make sure that you complete each section neatly and completely.

FOCUS

Ask a teacher, parent, or friend to review your practice applications.

Do your best to complete each application as well as you are able. After you are done, ask someone else to look over your completed application samples and suggest any improvements.

APPLICATION FOR EMPLOYMENT

_____ / _____ / _____
Date of Application

As an equal opportunity employer, this company does not discriminate in hiring or terms and conditions of employment because of an individual's race, creed, color, sex, age, disability, religion, or national origin.

━━━ AVAILABILITY ━━━

Position Applying for:_____ Date Available to Start:_____

Salary Desired:_____

Desired Schedule: Check Days Available: ☐ Sun   ☐ Mon   ☐ Tue   ☐ Wed   ☐ Thur   ☐ Fri   ☐ Sat

☐ Full-Time   ☐ Part-Time   ☐ Temporary   Hours Available Each Day: _____ _____ _____ _____ _____ _____ _____

━━━ PERSONAL INFORMATION ━━━

Last Name	First Name	Middle Name	
Present Street Address	City	State	Zip
Previous Street Address	City	State	Zip
Daytime Telephone No. ( )	Evening Telephone No. ( )	Social Security Number	Are you over 18?

━━━ EMPLOYMENT HISTORY ━━━

List employment starting with your _most recent_ position. Account for any time during this period in which you were unemployed by stating the nature of your activities. If you have no prior employment history, include personal references to be contacted.

May we contact your present employer?   ☐ YES   ☐ NO

Employer	Dates		Position/Title
	From	To	
Address			Duties Performed
City State Telephone ( )			
Supervisor	Hourly Rate/Salary		
	Starting	Final	
Reason for Leaving			

Employer	Dates		Position/Title
	From	To	
Address			Duties Performed
City State Telephone ( )			
Supervisor	Hourly Rate/Salary		
	Starting	Final	
Reason for Leaving			

Employer	Dates		Position/Title
	From	To	
Address			Duties Performed
City State Telephone ( )			
Supervisor	Hourly Rate/Salary		
	Starting	Final	
Reason for Leaving			

Employer	Dates		Position/Title
	From	To	
Address			Duties Performed
City State Telephone ( )			
Supervisor	Hourly Rate/Salary		
	Starting	Final	
Reason for Leaving			

EDUCATION

Type of School	Name and Location of School		Degree / Area of Study	Number of Years Completed	Graduated? (check one)
High School	Name				☐ Yes ☐ No
	City	State			GPA_____
College	Name				☐ Yes ☐ No
	City	State			GPA_____
Other	Name				☐ Yes ☐ No
	City	State			GPA_____

SPECIAL SKILLS

☐ Typing   ☐ Lotus   ☐ Word Processing   ☐ 10 Key (by touch) Applicable Skills or Equipment Operated:

_____wpm   _____keystrokes   _____

ACADEMIC AND PROFESSIONAL ACTIVITIES AND ACHIEVEMENTS

Academic and Professional Activities and Achievements, Awards, Publications, or Technical-Professional Societies. Indicate type or name. Exclude organizations which indicate race, creed, color, sex, age, religion, disability, or national origin of its members.	Date Awarded

MISCELLANEOUS

Is there any additional information involving a change of your name or assumed name that will permit us to check your record? If yes, please explain.

Have you ever been employed by this company or any of its divisions? ☐ Yes ☐ No	Dates Employed	Which Division?	Supervisor	Position

List names of friends or relatives now employed by this company.

Have you ever been convicted of a crime? ☐ Yes ☐ No (conviction of a crime does not automatically disqualify an applicant from consideration) If yes, please explain:

Are there any jobs for which you do not wish to be considered? Please explain.

PERSON TO CONTACT IN CASE OF EMERGENCY

This information is to facilitate contact in the event of an emergency and is not used in the selection process.

Full Name	Address	Phone	Relationship to you?
Place of Employment	Address	Phone	

PLEASE READ THIS STATEMENT CAREFULLY

I hereby affirm that the information given by me on this application for employment is complete and accurate. I understand that any falsification will be immediate grounds for dismissal. I authorize a thorough investigation to be made in connection with this application concerning my character, general reputation, personal characteristics, employment, educational background, and criminal record, whichever may be applicable. I understand that this investigation may include personal interviews with third parties such as family members, business associates, financial sources, friends, neighbors, and others with whom I am acquainted.

It is my understanding that as a prerequisite to consideration for employment, I must agree to submit to any post-employment examinations, physical or other, as the Company may lawfully require. The Company will pay the reasonable cost of any such examination which may be required.

I understand and agree that any falsification or omission either on this form or in my response to questions asked during any interview or other examination process is grounds for immediate termination of my employment no matter when the falsification or omission is discovered.

If I am hired, I agree that my employment and compensation can be terminated with or without cause and without notice at any time, at the option of this company or myself. I understand that no representative of this company other than a Vice President has authority to enter into any agreement for any specified period of time or to make any agreement contrary to the foregoing. I further understand that I have the right to make a written request within a reasonable period of time for a complete and accurate disclosure of the nature and scope of the investigation.

I have read and affirm as my own the above statements.

Signature_____ Date_____

APPLICANTS IN THE STATE OF MARYLAND ONLY

Under Maryland law an employer may not require or demand any applicant for employment or prospective employment or any employee to submit to or take a polygraph, lie detector, or similar test or examination as a condition of employment or continued employment. Any employer who violates this provision is guilty of a misdemeanor and subject to a fine not to exceed $100.

Signature_____ Date_____

APPLICANTS IN THE STATE OF MASSACHUSETTS ONLY

It is unlawful in Massachusetts to require or administer a lie detector test as a condition of employment or continued employment. An employer who violates this law shall be subject to criminal penalties and civil liability.

Signature_____ Date_____

APPLICATION FOR EMPLOYMENT

AN EQUAL OPPORTUNITY EMPLOYER

INSTRUCTIONS: 1. *Please type or print legibly in black ink.*
2. *All areas must be completed for consideration.*
3. ***Return completed form to the agency specified on the Job Bank by the closing date.***

TITLE OF POSITION AND CLASS CODE	
AGENCY NAME	
POSTING NUMBER	**REFERENCE SOURCE**

MARK TYPE(S) OF EMPLOYMENT ACCEPTABLE TO YOU

☐ Full-time ☐ Part-time ☐ Temporary

PRIVACY NOTICE	The State is requesting your Social Security number under authority of IC 4-1-8 to accomplish statutory purposes. Disclosure is mandatory and this form cannot be processed without it.	Social Security number

Name of applicant (last, first, middle)

Mailing address (number and street, city or town, state, ZIP code)

Area code and telephone number	Date of birth (*if under 18 years*)	County of residence
Home ( ) Other ( )		

CRIMINAL RECORD

Have you ever been convicted of a crime, other than minor traffic violations?
If yes, provide information regarding the conviction (*offense, date, sentence*) on a separate, attached sheet.
☐ Yes ☐ No

NOTICE: A "Yes" response will not necessarily eliminate you from consideration for employment.

EDUCATIONAL EXPERIENCE

Please circle the highest grade completed.   1 2 3 4 5 6 7 8
9 10 11 12 13 14 15 16 16+

Do you have a GED certificate?   ☐ Yes ☐ No

List below all high schools and post high schools attended. A copy of applicable transcripts **may be required** at the time of the interview.

NAME AND LOCATION OF SCHOOL	FROM MO.	FROM YR.	TO MO.	TO YR.	FIELDS OF STUDY (*major, minor*)	NUMBER SEMESTER HOURS COMPLETED	NUMBER QUARTER HOURS COMPLETED	DIPLOMA, CERTIFICATE OR TYPE OF DEGREE

SPECIALIZED TRAINING OR CLASSES RELEVANT TO THE JOB

INSTITUTES / SEMINARS OR TITLES OF SPECIAL COURSES	COMPANY / SPONSOR / SCHOOL	DATES ATTENDED	SKILLS ACQUIRED / CREDITS EARNED

PROFESSIONAL CERTIFICATION	STATUS	PERSONNEL USE ONLY	
Are you currently certified, registered, or licensed in any profession? (*If yes, give complete information, including any license or registration number, and attach a copy of certificate if related to the position for which you are applying.*) ☐ Yes ☐ No	Are you currently a State employee? ☐ Yes ☐ No	Typing score	Date administered
License or registration number	Date of issue (*mo./yr.*)	Have you been previously employed by the State? ☐ Yes ☐ No	Agency
	Expiration date	Dates employed	Verified by

EXAMINATION SCHEDULING FOR APPLICABLE MERIT POSITIONS

Your application will be reviewed to determine if you meet the required minimum qualifications of the position for which you are applying. If these are met and the position also requires a written exam, you will receive notification prior to the examination, indicating the date, time and place. Unless otherwise indicated below, the location will be the test site closest to your residence.

☐ I request the following testing location: _____

IMPORTANT NOTICE: Failure to appear for a scheduled exam without prior notice will result in your application being inactivated.

Name of applicant (*last, first, middle*)

WORK EXPERIENCE

1. List below, beginning with your most recent position, **all of your work experience**, including military service (*specify highest rank held*) and all volunteer activities. Attach additional 8-1/2" x 11" sheets if necessary.
2. **If your title and duties changed substantially in the course of your service in any one organization, indicate such changes clearly and as separate employment.**
3. Be sure to include current employment.
4. **Experience that cannot be confirmed is not acceptable.**
5. **Please do not submit a resume for this portion of the application.**

Title of present or previous job	From (*mo., day, yr.*)	To (*mo., day, yr.*)	Approximate number of hours worked per week
Name of employer / organization and address (*number and street, city, state, ZIP code*)			Telephone number (*area code*)
Name of supervisor / title	Number and job types of the employees you supervised (*if any*). [*Example: 3 managers, 2 clerks*]		

Describe the duties of your position in the order of importance. Indicate what machinery or office equipment was utilized.

Reason for leaving	Final salary
	$ per

Title of previous job	From (*mo., day, yr.*)	To (*mo., day, yr.*)	Approximate number of hours worked per week
Name of employer / organization and address (*number and street, city, state, ZIP code*)			Telephone number (*area code*)
Name of supervisor / title	Number and job types of the employees you supervised (*if any*). [*Example: 3 managers, 2 clerks*]		

Describe the duties of your position in the order of importance. Indicate what machinery or office equipment was utilized.

Reason for leaving	Final salary
	$ per

Title of previous job	From (*mo., day, yr.*)	To (*mo., day, yr.*)	Approximate number of hours worked per week
Name of employer / organization and address (*number and street, city, state, ZIP code*)			Telephone number (*area code*)
Name of supervisor / title	Number and job types of the employees you supervised (*if any*). [*Example: 3 managers, 2 clerks*]		

Describe the duties of your position in the order of importance. Indicate what machinery or office equipment was utilized.

Reason for leaving	Final salary
	$ per

Have you ever been discharged by any employer?
☐ Yes   ☐ No

REFERENCES (*Please do not list relatives as references*)

Name of reference	Telephone number (*Area code*) ( )
Address (*number and street, city, state, ZIP code*)	

Name of reference	Telephone number (*Area code*) ( )
Address (*number and street, city, state, ZIP code*)	

Name of reference	Telephone number (*Area code*) ( )
Address (*number and street, city, state, ZIP code*)	

Name of reference	Telephone number (*Area code*) ( )
Address (*number and street, city, state, ZIP code*)	

VETERAN PREFERENCE FOR MERIT POSITIONS

If you wish to claim Veteran's Preference Points, please indicate the applicable eligibility below and submit the required documentation with your application. Preference points will not be granted unless the documentation is submitted with your application.

☐ Veteran (*Submit DD Form 214*)

☐ War Veteran (*Submit DD Form 214*)

☐ Disabled Veteran (*Submit DD Form 214 and Disability Claim Certificate*)

☐ Spouse of Disabled Veteran (*Submit DD Form 214, Disability Claim Certificate, and Marriage Certificate*)

☐ Unremarried Spouse of Deceased Veteran (*Submit DD form 214, Marriage Certificate, and Death Certificate*)

MILITARY STATUS

☐ Active	Branch		
☐ Discharged	Rank		
☐ Reserve	Entry date	Exit date	

CERTIFICATE OF APPLICANT AND AUTHORIZATION OF REFERENCE AND / OR EMPLOYMENT VERIFICATION

I certify that there are no misrepresentations in or falsifications of these statements and answers. I am aware that should investigations disclose such, my application may be disqualified, my name removed from all eligible lists, and my future applications may not be accepted. I am also aware that falsification of this application, or any accompanying data, may result in my dismissal from any position in State employment. I authorize any person, agency, partnership, or corporation having any information concerning my background, educational record, or employment record to release such information. This information is to be used for possible employment with the State.

Signature of applicant	Date signed

PRIVACY NOTICE	The State is requesting your Social Security number under authority of IC 4-1-8 to accomplish statutory purposes. Disclosure is mandatory and this form cannot be processed without it.	Social Security number

EQUAL EMPLOYMENT OPPORTUNITY INFORMATION

The following information is requested in order to ensure equal employment opportunity and for record keeping purposes only. Disclosure is completely voluntary. Your application will not be rejected if you choose not to disclose the requested information. If you choose to disclose the following information, it will not be used to discriminate against you in the employment process.

PART 1 - RACE

Check one:

☐ White ☐ Hispanic ☐ Asian or Pacific Islander

☐ Black ☐ American Indian or Alaskan Native ☐ Other *(specify)* _____

PART 2 - SEX (*GENDER*)   **PART 3 - AGE**

Check one:

☐ Male ☐ Female   Are you over 40?   ☐ Yes   ☐ No

PART 4 - DISABILITY

The government defines an individual with a disability as any person who:

1. has a physical or mental impairment that substantially limits one or more major life activities *(e.g. seeing, hearing, working)*;
2. has a record of such impairment; or
3. is regarded as having such an impairment.

In accordance with this definition, do you regard yourself as an individual with a disability?   ☐ Yes   ☐ No

Application for Employment

We are an equal opportunity employer and do not unlawfully discriminate in employment. No question on this application is used for the purpose of limiting or excluding any applicant from consideration for employment on a basis prohibited by local, state, or federal law. Equal access to employment, services, and programs is available to all persons. Those applicants requiring reasonable accommodation to the application and/or interview process should notify a representative of the organization.

Applicant name: _____ Date: _____

Position(s) applied for or type of work desired: _____

_____

_____

Address: _____

Telephone #: _____ Social Security #: _____

Type of employment desired: _____ full-time _____ part-time _____ temporary

Date you will be available to start work: _____

Are you able to meet the attendance requirements? _____ Yes _____ No

Do you have any objection to working overtime if necessary? _____ Yes _____ No

Can you travel if required by this position? _____ Yes _____ No

Have you ever been previously employed by our organization? _____ Yes _____ No

Can you submit proof of legal employment authorization and identity? _____ Yes _____ No

Have you ever been convicted of a crime in the last 7 years? _____ Yes _____ No

If yes, please explain (a conviction will not automatically bar employment): _____

_____

_____

_____

Drivers license number: _____

How were you referred to us? _____

_____

_____

EMPLOYMENT HISTORY

Please provide all employment information for your past 10 years of employers starting with the most recent.

Employer: _____ Position held: _____

Address: _____ Telephone #: _____

Immediate supervisor and title: _____

Dates employed: from _____ to_____ Salary: _____

Job summary: _____

Reason for leaving: _____

Employer: _____ Position held: _____

Address: _____ Telephone #: _____

Immediate supervisor and title: _____

Dates employed: from _____ to_____ Salary: _____

Job summary: _____

Reason for leaving: _____

Employer: _____ Position held: _____

Address: _____ Telephone #: _____

Immediate supervisor and title: _____

Dates employed: from _____ to_____ Salary: _____

Job summary: _____

Reason for leaving: _____

Employer: _____ Position held: _____

Address: _____ Telephone #: _____

Immediate supervisor and title: _____

Dates employed: from _____ to_____ Salary: _____

Job summary: _____

Reason for leaving: _____

OTHER SKILLS AND QUALIFICATIONS

Summarize any job-related training, skills, licenses, certificates, and/or other qualifications:

_____

_____

_____

EDUCATIONAL HISTORY

List school name and location, years completed, course of study, and any degrees earned:

High School:_____

College: _____

Technical Training: _____

Other: _____

REFERENCES

List 3 references names, telephone numbers, and years known (do not include relatives or employers):

_____

_____

_____

I hereby authorize the potential employer to contact, obtain, and verify the accuracy of information contained in this application from all previous employers, educational institutions, and references. I also hereby release from liability the potential employer and its representatives for seeking, gathering, and using such information to make employment decisions and all other persons or organizations for providing such information.

I understand that any misrepresentation or material omission made by me on this application will be sufficient cause for cancellation of this application or immediate termination of employment if I am employed, whenever it may be discovered.

If I am employed, I acknowledge that there is no specified length of employment and that this application does not constitute an agreement or contract for employment. Accordingly, either I or the employer can terminate the relationship at will, with or without cause, at any time, so long as there is no violation of applicable federal or state law.

I understand that it is the policy of this organization not to refuse to hire or otherwise discriminate against a qualified individual with a disability because of that persons need for a reasonable accommodation as required by the ADA.

I also understand that if I am employed, I will be required to provide satisfactory proof of identity and legal work authorization within three days of being hired. Failure to submit such proof within the required time shall result in immediate termination of employment.

I represent and warrant that I have read and fully understand the foregoing and that I seek employment under these conditions.

_____   _____
Applicant Signature   Date

CONCLUSION: CREATE A GOOD IMPRESSION WITH YOUR APPLICATION

You have learned how an application is often used to screen people out of a job. You have also learned how to create an inventory of information and to use it to fill out an application.

But getting a job involves more than filling out applications. To get a job, you have to know what sort of job you want and what skills you have to do it. Plus, you have to get interviews. Many jobs will also require you to get more education or training.

Many employers will ask you to fill out an application during your job search. For this reason, it is important that you know how to use one to create a positive impression.

We hope that the information in Part 3 has helped you understand how applications are used in the job search.

Part 4

Why Should I Hire You?

- Chapter 16: What Is an Interview?
- Chapter 17: What an Employer Expects
- Chapter 18: Three-Step Process for Answering Interview Questions—Giving the Right Clues
- Chapter 19: Build Confidence for Your Interviews
- Chapter 20: Get Ready for the Interview and Your New Job

Most people are afraid of job interviews. We agree that most job interviews are not fun. Employers are often trying to find out why they should *not* hire you. They want to hire the best person for the job. If more than one person is applying for a job, an employer must eliminate all applicants except for the one to be hired.

An employer's task, then, is to find reasons you are not the best person for the job. Since an employer usually doesn't know you, he or she has to depend on just a few things when deciding:

- Written information (such as resumes and applications)
- Information from past employers and references
- The interview

An interview usually lasts an hour or less. These 60 minutes are the most important time you spend in the job search process. In fact, most interviewers form an impression of you within the first few minutes of an interview. If their impression is negative, you have a very small chance of getting a job offer.

Part 4 of this book is about improving how you handle the job interview. It will help you create the positive first impression that is so important. It will teach you how to present your skills and handle problem questions. Most importantly, it will help you learn how to answer that most important interview question: "Why should I hire you?"

If you think about it, "Why should I hire you?" is the most important question an employer can ask. Even if an interviewer doesn't ask this question out loud or exactly in this way, it is *the* question that every employer must consider. If you can't tell employers why they *should* hire you over someone else, you have little chance of getting hired.

If you can present an answer that is both true and convincing, you will have a big advantage over other job seekers who can't. It's that simple.

chapter 16

What Is an Interview?

THE GOALS OF THIS CHAPTER ARE

- To understand the purpose of an interview
- To understand the good-worker traits employers want
- To make sure that you can state your job objective clearly

DON'T WAIT FOR THE JOB TO OPEN!

People usually think of an interview as a meeting with an employer who has a job opening. You find out about a job opening, and you call to set up an interview.

But you don't have to wait until you hear about a job opening. You can get an interview even if an employer doesn't have a job opening now.

Read the story that follows. It will show you why it's good to get interviews whether or not there is a job opening. Then answer the questions that follow the story.

EXAMPLE

Making a Good Impression Pays Off Later

Kim Taylor is a restaurant manager. She is in her office and working at her desk. Someone knocks on her door. Assistant manager Mark Hoffman enters.

Mark: (Looking worried.) I came to tell you that Bill Jones in the kitchen just quit. Do you want me to put an ad in the paper tomorrow? We can't afford to be understaffed in the kitchen.

Kim: No, hold off on the ad. Someone came in here a few weeks ago—let's see, what was her name? Mullins? No, Marilyn. That's it. Marilyn Gilbert.

Mark: Marilyn Gilbert? I remember her.

Kim: (She opens a drawer in her desk and pulls out a file folder.) I wrote her name down and put it in a file. I was really impressed with her. Let's give her a call and see if she's still looking for work. I've got a few other people in mind, too, if she's not available.

Mark: That's great. It will save us a lot of time and trouble if we don't have to advertise.

Kim (Smiling.): That's the idea.

The job seeker, Marilyn Gilbert, knew there were no job openings when she came in. But Marilyn asked for an interview anyway. She hoped to make a positive impression on the manager in case a job opened up. Marilyn did make a good impression. As a result, Marilyn was the first person the manager thought of to replace a worker who was leaving.

---

 think about it

Think about the importance of making a good impression during an interview. Answer these questions.

1. Why did the assistant manager, Mark Hoffman, seem worried when an employee quit?

_____

_____

_____

_____

2. Why did Kim Taylor, the manager, think of Marilyn Gilbert when she found out there was a job to be filled?

_____

_____

_____

_____

3. Why would both managers be pleased about hiring Marilyn, rather than advertising the job opening?

_____

_____

_____

_____

INTERVIEWING NOW MAY SAVE AN EMPLOYER TIME AND MONEY

Employers like to save money on advertising. They also like to make the hiring process go as smoothly as possible. You can save employers time and money if you present yourself as a possible worker now or for the future.

Don't wait for a job opening. Talk to potential employers before a job opens up. This is also considered an interview. When a job is available later, an employer might hire you without running an ad.

This can happen _if_ you make a good impression and possess good-worker traits. Part 4 shows you how to make a good impression in your job interviews. It will also help you get the job you want.

> ## FOCUS
>
> _An interview is a chance to talk with someone who hires people with skills like yours._

GOOD-WORKER TRAITS

Good-worker traits are the skills that make you a good worker. All employers look for people with these skills.

Some examples of good-worker traits are the following:

- Getting to work every day on time
- Honesty
- Getting the job done
- Getting along with co-workers
- Working hard

Often, employers won't hire a person who does not have or use these skills.

KNOW YOUR JOB OBJECTIVE

Be sure you know what your job objective is before you begin the interview process. Examples of job objectives are "a responsible position in retail sales" or "a position working with preschool children that requires dedication and high energy."

Do You Know Your Job Objective?

Answer the questions that follow to see if you do. Check Yes or No in the box beside each question.

Job Objective Factors	Yes	No
I know what kind of work I want to do.	☐	☐
I know what skills I need to do this work.	☐	☐
I know what kind of work matches my training and experience.	☐	☐
I know the work environment I like (indoor, outdoor, noisy, quiet, busy, slow, and so on).	☐	☐
I know what wages or salary I need to earn and what this kind of work pays.	☐	☐

If you answered "No" to any of the questions, your job objective is not clear enough yet. You need to spend more time figuring out the sort of job you want and the skills you need to do it. Do this before you begin interviewing for a job.

✔ checkpoint

Answer the questions that follow to review what you have learned in this chapter.

1. What is an interview?

_____

_____

_____

2. Why do employers look for good-worker traits?

_____

_____

_____

3. Why is it important to know your job objective?

_____

_____

_____

challenge: List "Good Worker" Traits

You are the owner of a small business. Your success depends on the kinds of workers you employ to keep the business running smoothly. You decide to post a notice on an employee bulletin board. The notice lists the "good worker" traits that you value most.

What traits are on your list? Write these traits on the notice here.

Hint: Think about what it takes for people to work together to accomplish a goal or a task.

NOTICE TO EMPLOYEES

Please Observe the Following Requirements:

_____

_____

_____

_____

_____

_____

_____

chapter 17

What an Employer Expects

THE GOALS OF THIS CHAPTER ARE

- To understand what an employer expects of you
- To learn how to meet those expectations

EMPLOYERS WANT SOLID EVIDENCE

When you go to an interview, you meet with someone who gathers information about you. Interviewers are like private detectives. They look for evidence that shows whether you are the right person for the job. To find the evidence, interviewers look for certain clues.

If they find the evidence they are looking for, you might be hired. If the interviewer doesn't find the right evidence, you will be screened out.

Many people feel nervous about going to interviews. But if you know how to give the right impression, or "evidence," you can go to an interview with more confidence.

THREE CLUES THAT EMPLOYERS LOOK FOR IN INTERVIEWS

Here are three clues most employers look for in the people they interview:

1. Do they make a good first impression?
2. Are they reliable?
3. Can they do the job?

Clue 1: Do They Make a Good First Impression?

Many individuals feel that it's not fair to judge people by their appearance. Fair or not, it happens anyway. How you look and how you act tell an interviewer a lot about your self-respect. How you present yourself also shows how much you pay attention to detail.

Dress and Grooming

What you wear to an interview depends on what kind of job you want. There is no standard uniform that works for every job interview. An office worker would not wear the same kind of clothing as a construction worker. The best rule to follow for what to wear on an interview is to dress like you think your supervisor would dress, but neater.

> **FOCUS**
>
> For an interview, dress like your supervisor would dress—but neater.

If you are not sure how the supervisor would dress, ask around. Ask parents, friends, teachers, and others. Avoid clothes that are either too casual or too dressy for the job. Remember, you want to make the very best impression possible.

Pay attention to details of appearance and personal hygiene. Such details include the following:

- Neat hairstyle

- Fingernails clean and trimmed

- Shoes shined

- Clothes clean, pressed, and conservative (not trendy)

- Makeup not too heavy

- Firm handshake and good eye contact

- No perfume or cologne (or very light)

Job seekers are often told to offer the interviewer a firm handshake at the start and end of the interview. They are also told to make plenty of eye contact.

Do what makes you feel comfortable. A handshake is a good idea if you can do it with confidence. Looking directly into someone's eyes can make you feel more nervous if you aren't used to it.

Try practicing these things with a friend or family member before an interview. Practice will make you feel more confident.

Posture and Personal Habits

Posture is another way to give positive clues about yourself. Sit up straight or lean forward a little. Look interested.

Try to keep your hands still. Don't gesture a lot or use nervous habits.

Smile when you get the chance, and don't chew gum. Also, don't smoke, even if the interviewer says you can.

Clue 2: Are They Reliable?

During the interview, look for chances to tell the interviewer how reliable you are. Those chances will come when the interviewer asks you questions. You will learn more about how to answer interview questions in Chapter 18.

During the interview, an employer will try to find out if you will do the following:

- Show up for work on time
- Get along well with other employees
- Get things done on time
- Show that you can be trusted

> **FOCUS**
>
> *One way to show an employer that you are reliable is to be on time for the interview.*

Clue 3: Can They Do the Job?

An employer will look for clues that prove you have the skills, training, or experience to handle the job. For entry-level jobs, you might not need experience or training. But you must show that you can learn to do the job.

Again, the questions you are asked during the interview will be your chance to show that you have the skills to learn the job.

The story that follows is about the second interview between Kim Taylor, the restaurant manager, and Marilyn Gilbert, the job seeker.

Mrs. Taylor called Marilyn to see if she still was looking for a job. They arranged another interview.

> **FOCUS**
>
> *If you give the right clues in an interview, you stand a good chance of getting the job.*

EXAMPLE

Selling Yourself—"Clinching the Deal"

During her previous interview with Mrs. Taylor, Marilyn had noticed that the manager wore slacks and a blouse on the job. Marilyn followed the rule about dressing like the supervisor.

For this interview, she wore dress slacks and a nice blouse. Her shoes matched her slacks.

Mrs. Taylor and Marilyn are talking in Mrs. Taylor's office. Marilyn answers Mrs. Taylor's questions carefully. Notice how she finds ways to talk about her skills.

Mrs. Taylor: Hello, Miss Gilbert. I'm glad you could meet with me today. Won't you sit down?

Marilyn: Thank you. I'm glad to be here, too.

Mrs. Taylor: Although we spoke a few weeks ago, I'd like to ask you a few more questions. Why are you interested in this job?

Marilyn: This job would require me to use my best skills, which are cooking and working under pressure. I like the challenge of working fast but still doing the job right. I know that in a restaurant customers want their food fast. And they want it to taste good.

Mrs. Taylor: It sounds as though you have worked for a restaurant before. What is your experience?

Marilyn: I don't have actual experience in a restaurant, but I am the oldest of six children. My mother has worked full time for years, and I've often been in charge of making the meals for my brothers and sisters.

Keeping everybody happy and well-fed has been one of my main responsibilities at home. And, of course, they like to bring their friends over sometimes too! Our relatives in the area come over for big Sunday dinners, so I've cooked for a crowd many times.

Mrs. Taylor: Have you ever had any other kind of training for this work?

Marilyn: I have taken classes in school related to cooking, and last year I attended a day-long seminar that was put on by a local catering company.

It was about catering for special parties and events, and planning the stages of a meal. We learned some special recipes and cooking tips, too.

Mrs. Taylor: You mentioned that cooking at home for your brothers and sisters was one of your main responsibilities. What would happen if your work hours conflicted with your work at home?

Marilyn: Of course I take my responsibilities at home seriously. But I never make an outside commitment unless I have worked out ways to keep that commitment.

My mother and I have discussed this thoroughly. We have made arrangements for the children when I work. Also, they are getting old enough now to take more care of themselves.

After a few more questions, Mrs. Taylor offered Marilyn the job. Then they talked about Marilyn's wages and work hours.

 think about it

Think about what an employer expects of you during an interview. Answer these questions.

1. What are some ways to give an interviewer positive clues about yourself?

   _____

   _____

   _____

   _____

2. Do you have an "interview outfit" or two ready? What will you wear?

   _____

   _____

   _____

   _____

3. In her interview with Mrs. Taylor, Marilyn gave examples to support her skills. Name some examples Marilyn used to support her skills.

_____

_____

_____

_____

✔ **checkpoint**

Answer the questions that follow to review what you have learned in this chapter.

1. What three clues does an employer look for during an interview?

_____

_____

_____

_____

2. What negative clues could an interviewee give during an interview?

_____

_____

_____

_____

challenge: See Yourself Through an Interviewer's Eyes

Imagine the following situation: You have just interviewed for a job. The person who interviewed you sends a memo about you to other people in the company who will be deciding who to hire for the job.

What would you want the memo to say about you? Write the memo in the following space from the point of view of the person who interviewed you.

Hint: Remember the three kinds of clues an employer looks for. Comments on these clues are likely to be the main part of the memo.

MEMORANDUM

TO: _____

FROM: _____

DATE: _____

SUBJECT: _____

Comments:

_____

_____

_____

_____

_____

_____

_____

_____

---

chapter 18

Three-Step Process for Answering Interview Questions—Giving the Right Clues

THE GOALS OF THIS CHAPTER ARE

- To learn a process for handling any interview question you might be asked
- To practice answering the most common (and hardest) interview questions

HANDLING INTERVIEW QUESTIONS

The most important part of the interview is how you answer questions. No book can tell you exactly what questions will be asked. But you can learn how to handle most questions that come your way.

We have said that an interviewer is like a detective looking for clues. Remember, the interviewer is watching for these clues you give about yourself:

- Do you present yourself well?

- Can you do the job?
- Are you reliable?

An interview is also a test of your communications skills. Communicating involves listening and talking. The process you learn about in this chapter shows you how to listen and talk effectively during an interview.

FOCUS

The best way to answer interview questions is to understand what clues the employer is looking for.

The Three-Step Process for Answering Interview Questions

Here are the three steps you can use in answering most interview questions. Following the steps is a sample interview question and how the Three-Step Process can be used to answer it.

- **Step 1:** Understand what is really being asked.
- **Step 2:** Present the facts to make yourself look good.
- **Step 3:** Give examples to support your best skills.

Sample Interview Question: How Will You Get to Work If You Take This Job?

Step 1: Understand What Is Really Being Asked

If you don't think about what the interviewer is really asking, you might answer, "I'll drive my car," "I'll take the bus," or "My Aunt Nancy will give me a lift." But the interviewer doesn't really care how you will get to work.

What the interviewer does care about is whether you have reliable transportation so that you can be on time to work every day. In other words, the question is "Are you reliable?" Now that you know what clue the interviewer is looking for, move on to Step 2.

Step 2: Present the Facts to Make Yourself Look Good

Use each interview question to bring out something positive about yourself. Go back to the sample question, "How will you get to work?" You could say, "I don't have a car, but I live two blocks from the bus line. The bus always runs, and I never have to worry about my car not starting on cold mornings!"

With that answer, you have told the interviewer not to worry. You have a reliable way to get to work on time. Besides answering the interviewer's real concern, you can make your answer even better. Step 3 shows you how.

Step 3: Give Examples to Support Your Skills

You might not realize it, but the ability to be on time for an appointment or for work is a skill. It's one thing to say, "I'm always on time." But you will make a bigger impression on the interviewer if you can give an example.

Go back to the sample question, "How will you get to work?" You could say, "I've always made a habit of being on time when I have made a commitment. When I was in school, I was always on time for my classes."

GOOD LISTENING HELPS YOU GIVE GOOD ANSWERS

The question "How will you get to work?" seemed simple enough. But with the Three-Step Process you just learned, you can make a question like that work for you. Here is the entire answer you could give. See how much more this answer accomplishes than simply saying, "I'll take the bus"?

> *"I don't have a car, but I live just two blocks from the bus line. I've been using the bus for a long time, and I never have to worry about my car not starting on cold mornings! And, of course, I've always made it a habit to be on time when I make a commitment. When I was in school, I was always on time for my classes."*

PRACTICING THE THREE-STEP PROCESS FOR ANSWERING INTERVIEW QUESTIONS

Practice answering interview questions using the Three-Step Process. You need practice because you won't have 10 minutes to think about every answer during the interview. Once you get the hang of it, your answers will come more quickly to you and you will feel more confident.

Practicing Interviewing

Take as much time as you need to think about each part of each question. Each of the following questions is one that job seekers find hard to answer. These questions are also often asked in interviews.

Sample Question 1: What Kind of Training or Experience Do You Have for This Job?

Step 1: What is really being asked?

_____

_____

_____

_____

Step 2: How can you use this question to make yourself look good?

_____

_____

_____

_____

Step 3: What are some examples you can give to support your skills? (Hint: If you have training or experience, don't be modest! If you don't, then let the interviewer know that you are eager and willing to learn.)

_____

_____

_____

_____

Now write your answer to Sample Question 1.

_____

_____

_____

_____

_____

_____

(continued)

(continued)

Sample Question 2: Can You Tell Me a Little About Yourself?

Step 1: What is really being asked?

_____

_____

_____

_____

Step 2: How can you use this question to make yourself look good?

_____

_____

_____

_____

Step 3: What are some examples you can give to support your skills? (*Hint:* Use this question to talk about your accomplishments such as good grades, past job experience, or other successes.)

_____

_____

_____

_____

Now write your answer to Sample Question 2.

_____

_____

_____

_____

_____

Sample Question 3: Why Do You Want This Job?

Step 1: What is really being asked?

_____

_____

_____

_____

Step 2: How can you use this question to make yourself look good?

_____

_____

_____

_____

Step 3: What are some examples you can give to support your skills? (*Hint:* Use this question to explain what you have to offer the business or organization. Don't talk about what you want the company to give you.)

_____

_____

_____

_____

Now write your answer to Sample Question 3.

_____

_____

_____

_____

_____

(continued)

(continued)

Sample Question 4: Why Should I Hire You?

This is *the* most important question for you to answer well in the interview!

Step 1: What is really being asked?

_____

_____

_____

_____

Step 2: How can you use this question to make yourself look good?

_____

_____

_____

_____

Step 3: What are some examples you can give to support your skills? (*Hint:* Use this question as a chance to point out your very best skills.)

_____

_____

_____

_____

Now write your answer to Sample Question 4.

_____

_____

_____

_____

_____

Sample Question 5: What Are Your Strongest Skills for This Job?

Step 1: What is really being asked?

_____

_____

_____

_____

Step 2: How can you use this question to make yourself look good?

_____

_____

_____

_____

Step 3: What are some examples you can give to support your skills? (*Hint:* The interviewer is giving you a chance to give strong clues about your good-worker traits. Again, don't be modest!)

_____

_____

_____

_____

Now write your answer to Sample Question 5.

_____

_____

_____

_____

_____

(continued)

(continued)

Sample Question 6: What Areas Are You Weak In?

Step 1: What is really being asked?

_____

_____

_____

_____

Step 2: How can you use this question to make yourself look good?

_____

_____

_____

Step 3: What are some examples you can give to support your skills? (*Hint:* Everyone has at least some weaknesses. A good response to this kind of question would be to talk about how you plan to improve.)

_____

_____

_____

Now write your answer to Sample Question 6.

_____

_____

_____

_____

_____

Sample Question 7: What Sorts of Problems Have You Had in Previous Jobs?

Step 1: What is really being asked?

_____

_____

_____

_____

Step 2: How can you use this question to make yourself look good? (_Hint:_ Do _not_ mention a major problem unless you can present yourself in a positive way. For example, "I have been called 'bossy' in a previous job, and it taught me how to better handle responsibility. I've learned to work better with a group now and get things done through cooperation.")

_____

_____

_____

Step 3: What are some examples you can give to support your skills? (_Hint:_ The ability to learn from mistakes or problems is an excellent skill. Use this question to show that you have a positive attitude toward solving problems. Don't put down former employers or co-workers.)

_____

_____

_____

Now write your answer to Sample Question 7.

_____

_____

_____

_____

_____

(continued)

(continued)

Sample Question 8: If We Hired You, How Would You Help Make Our Organization Better?

Step 1: What is really being asked?

_____

_____

_____

_____

Step 2: How can you use this question to make yourself look good?

_____

_____

_____

_____

Step 3: What are some examples you can give to support your skills? (*Hint:* This is another chance to show what you have to offer the employer.)

_____

_____

_____

_____

Now write your answer to Sample Question 8.

_____

_____

_____

_____

_____

Sample Question 9: If You Could Design a Perfect Job for Yourself, What Would That Be?

Step 1: What is really being asked?

_____

_____

_____

_____

Step 2: How can you use this question to make yourself look good?

_____

_____

_____

_____

Step 3: What are some examples you can give to support your skills? (_Hint:_ This is not the time to talk about becoming a famous rock star. Use this question to talk about how important it is to you to use your best skills in the work you do. Skills that, of course, you would be using in the job you are applying for.)

_____

_____

_____

_____

Now write your answer to Sample Question 9.

_____

_____

_____

_____

_____

(continued)

(continued)

Sample Question 10: How Well Do You Handle Responsibility?

Step 1: What is really being asked?

_____

_____

_____

_____

Step 2: How can you use this question to make yourself look good?

_____

_____

_____

Step 3: What are some examples you can give to support your skills? (*Hint:* Describe ways you have handled responsibility in the past and ways you have improved. You might say, "I do best when I take on more responsibility gradually, as I adjust to the job." This tells the interviewer that you won't take on more than you can handle. It also tells the interviewer that you are eager to improve.)

_____

_____

_____

_____

Now write your answer to Sample Question 10.

_____

_____

_____

_____

Sample Question 11: What Do You Like to Do in Your Spare Time?

Step 1: What is really being asked?

_____

_____

_____

_____

Step 2: How can you use this question to make yourself look good?

_____

_____

_____

_____

Step 3: What are some examples you can give to support your skills? (*Hint:* You don't have to—and shouldn't—give the interviewer a list of all the things you do when you are goofing off. Talk about one or two activities that show interests or skills related to the job you want.)

_____

_____

_____

_____

Now write your answer to Sample Question 11.

_____

_____

_____

_____

_____

THE QUESTION OF PAY

The Three-Step Process does not work well with one question. This is the question about what you want to be paid for the job you will do.

Find out before the interview what wages are typical for this job. Also, have a good idea what you need to earn. You should look for a job that will allow you to meet all your expenses.

The interviewer may ask, "What do you expect to be paid?" Try to avoid answering this question until you are offered the job. There are two reasons to avoid the question:

- First, you might expect too much. Then the employer will feel that you won't be satisfied with a lower wage.

- Second, you might name a lower wage than the employer planned to pay. Then you get the job, but you lose the better wage.

A good way to avoid answering "What do you expect to be paid?" is to ask a question in return, such as "What does this position pay?" Many employers will tell you.

However, some will insist that you answer the question. This is why it's so important to do some research and find out a typical salary for the job you want. If the interviewer insists that you answer the question, give a salary range that most similar jobs would pay.

RANGE OF PAY

If an employer insists on knowing your desired salary, you might give one of the ranges below:

- $7 to $9 an hour, or $9 to $12 an hour
- $200 to $300 per week, or $300 to $400 per week
- Lower to mid 20s per year

By giving a wide range of pay, you are less likely to be eliminated because you are asking too much or too little. Base your answer on what you think is fair and reasonable.

WHAT IF YOU CAN'T ANSWER AN INTERVIEW QUESTION?

Don't panic. If you are feeling very nervous, take a deep breath and count to 10. Concentrate on what the interviewer is saying. The problem might be that you simply did not understand the question.

If that happens, you can say, "I'm sorry, but I'm not sure I understand the question. Could you please say it another way?" Then listen very carefully, use the Three-Step Process, and do the best you can.

> ### FOCUS
>
> *Don't panic if you can't answer a question. Take a deep breath and ask the interviewer to state the question in a different way.*

 think about it

Think about the interviewing process. Answer these questions.

1. What key skills are involved in answering interview questions?

   _____

   _____

   _____

   _____

   _____

2. How much do you need to make on your next job to be able to meet your expenses? List your expenses so you remember them all.

   _____

   _____

   _____

   _____

3. Review the interview questions you answered. Are there any questions you still don't feel comfortable answering? Practice them now until you feel confident.

_____

_____

_____

_____

_____

✔ **checkpoint**

After completing this chapter, answer these questions. They will help you review what you just learned.

1. What are the three steps to answering interview questions?

_____

_____

_____

2. How should you handle the question of pay?

_____

_____

_____

3. What should you do if you can't answer an interview question?

_____

_____

_____

challenge: Answer the Most Important Question

Imagine that you are in an interview. The interviewer is going to ask you only one question. (In reality, this is very unlikely. But this is a question you *must* be prepared to answer, in one form or another.) The question is "Why should I hire you?" What will you say?

From all you have learned so far, give your best answer to the question. Why *should* an employer hire you for this job over someone else? Try to improve on the answer you gave in a previous section of this chapter.

Write your answer here.

_____

_____

_____

_____

_____

chapter 19

Build Confidence for Your Interviews

THE GOALS OF THIS CHAPTER ARE

- To feel confident in how you talk about yourself
- To learn how you can ask questions in the interview
- To learn what to do after an interview

AN INTERVIEW IS NO TIME TO BE MODEST

It should be clear by now that an interview is no time to be modest! Even if it feels like bragging, practice talking about your best points. Remember to support them with examples.

Employers won't hire you because you seem "nice." They will hire you if they believe you can do the job. How else can they know that if you don't tell them?

TALK ABOUT YOUR BEST POINTS AND SPEAK WITH SELF-CONFIDENCE

Employers look for people who can do the job. Even if you believe you can do the job, you must convince the employer to hire you. Having confidence in yourself will help you tell an employer about your skills for the job.

Speak with Confidence

Here is an exercise for you to do on speaking with confidence.

First, read the list of statements that follow. Put a check mark on the line beside each statement that sounds like something you might say.

Next, in the spaces following each statement, write a better version of the statement. Change each statement as much as you feel is necessary. Remember, you want to give the interviewer positive clues about yourself.

1. "I'm okay with my hands, I guess."

   _____

   _____

   _____

2. "I'm pretty good about getting places on time, most of the time."

   _____

   _____

   _____

3. "I don't really have any actual experience, but I'm pretty sure I can learn."

   _____

   _____

   _____

4. "I thought that maybe you'd have some kind of job for a person like me."

   _____

   _____

   _____

5. "I know I'm probably not as qualified as a lot of other people, but I really hope you'll give me a chance anyway."

   _____

(continued)

(continued)

_____

_____

6. "I guess I want this job because your ad made it sound like something I might be able to do."

_____

_____

_____

7. "Reliable? Yeah, I'm pretty reliable. I mean, it's not like I'd be calling in sick all the time, or anything like that."

_____

_____

_____

Tips for Speaking with Confidence

Here are some tips you can use to be more aware of how you speak about yourself.

- *Don't* put yourself down with negative statements like "I know I'm probably not as qualified as a lot of other people."

- *Don't* use weak words such as "pretty good," "I guess," "might be able to," "I thought that maybe," and so on. Don't apologize for your lack of experience. Instead, point to any life experience or training you can use to support your good-worker traits.

- *Do* use words that show you have faith in yourself. For example: "I am very good with my hands," "I am always on time," and "I believe your organization would benefit from having a person with my skills."

- *Do* answer the interviewer's real concern. Say positive things about yourself. For example: "Yes, I am reliable. I know how important it is to show up for work every day and do the job right."

Making Positive Statements

The statements that follow are similar to the ones you read in the previous worksheet. Can you see the difference? The earlier statements belong to a person who does not sound confident. This new set of statements, however, shows strength and self-esteem. If you were an employer, which type of person would you want to hire?

1. "One of my best skills is working with my hands."

2. "I always try to be on time, whatever the situation."

3. "I have had many experiences that needed the kind of skills I would use on this job. Let me give you some examples."

4. "I'd like to talk with you about the skills I have to offer your organization."

5. "I believe I have the skills needed to handle this job, and I'd be happy to have the chance to show you that."

6. "When I saw your advertisement, I knew I had the skills you were looking for."

7. "Yes, I consider myself a very reliable person. Let me give you some examples."

Speaking with self-confidence takes practice. You can practice every day, starting now. Notice how you talk about yourself in ordinary conversation. Most of us are not aware of our negative speech habits. Get used to using the language of self-confidence every day. Then you will not feel awkward when you use it in your interviews.

YOU CAN ASK QUESTIONS IN THE INTERVIEW, TOO

It's a good idea to find out about an organization before you interview for a job. You can do this by talking to people who work there. Or you can call the receptionist and ask some brief questions about the organization. A librarian can help you find information about a possible employer.

If you have access to the Internet, you can often find all sorts of information about an organization. Ask if the organization has a Web site. If so, log on to learn as much as you can.

But you might not be able to learn much about the job until you are actually in the interview. This next example will show how you can get information during an interview.

EXAMPLE

Asking Questions

Read what follows. Notice how the job seeker found ways to ask questions about the organization.

Interviewer: This job requires someone who can work fast and efficiently. Can you work under pressure?

Applicant: I actually work better under pressure. I like the challenge. How much volume do you do here on an average day?

Interviewer: We have a lot of different people who work here. Do you usually get along well with other employees?

Applicant: I think people work best together when they are willing to help each other out. How many employees do you have here?

You and the interviewer can both gather the kind of information you need for deciding whether you are right for the job and the job is right for you.

---

 think about it

Think about information you would like to gather about an organization or company where you would like to work.

What are some questions that would be important to ask in an interview?

_____

_____

_____

_____

CLOSING THE INTERVIEW

There are two things you should do at the end of an interview. If you want the job, the first thing to do is to say so. The second thing is to arrange for a time to call the employer back. You will call to find out if a decision has been made about hiring you. This is called the Call Back Close.

EXAMPLE

A Call Back Close

Read what follows. It shows you what we mean by a Call Back Close. This takes place at the end of an interview.

Interviewer (Rising from his chair.): Well, thank you very much for coming in, Miss Stevens. It's been nice talking with you.

Applicant: I've enjoyed meeting you, too, Mr. Glass. I want you to know that I am interested in this job. It is just what I have been looking for, and I would be willing to work hard to show you that I could do it. If I have any other questions, when could I call you? (Or, "When do you think you will make a decision?")

Make sure you get a day and time to call back. Then put that date on your calendar and call on time.

AFTER THE INTERVIEW—FOLLOW UP!

After the interview, plan to follow up. The term "follow up" refers to things you should do after you make contact with anyone in your job search network—especially employers. The first thing to do is to send a thank-you note. Then schedule follow-up phone calls. Remember the story about Marilyn Gilbert? In her case, the employer called her when a job opened.

> **FOCUS**
>
> *Following up after the interview is almost as important as the interview itself.*

Send Thank-You Notes and E-mails

Everyone likes to be recognized for being helpful. But a thank-you note or e-mail is more than a nice gesture—it's an excellent job search tool. Write thank-you notes or e-mails to anyone who helps you in your job search.

Send a paper thank-you note to an employer immediately after an interview. If you want, do this in addition to sending an e-mail after the interview. So few job seekers do this that you will make a very good impression. And the employer is likely to remember you when it comes time to make a decision about who to hire.

Here is an example of a thank-you note. Marilyn Gilbert sent this note to Mrs. Taylor, the restaurant manager, after their first interview.

November 30

Dear Mrs. Taylor:

I want to thank you for taking the time to meet with me recently. I was very impressed with your company and the state-of-the-art equipment your facility utilizes. I am very interested in this type of work and would be willing to work hard if you had a job opening in the future. I look forward to meeting with you again.

Sincerely,

Marilyn Gilbert

If you are wondering whether a thank-you note is worth the effort, remember Marilyn Gilbert. The manager of the restaurant said she had "a few other people in mind" for the job. But it was Marilyn's name she thought of first. Marilyn's thank-you note made a difference.

Tips for Writing Thank-You Notes

Follow these tips when you prepare a thank-you note for an employer.

- If you use e-mail, carefully write your e-mail thank-you note in advance. Make sure it has no grammar or spelling errors. Consider mailing a paper thank-you note too since mailed notes often get even more attention.

- Use nice stationery with a simple "Thank You" on the front. You can buy this at a stationery store. Beige, light gray, or off-white colors are best.

- Write it out by hand (unless your handwriting is hard to read) and mail it.

- Address the interviewer formally (Dear Mr. Brown, Dear Ms. Smith). Don't use first names.

- Keep the note short.

- Send the note right after the interview.

Call Back After the Interview

It is especially important to call back an employer after you make contact—for instance, if you have an interview. Call a few days or a week later to let the employer know you are still interested in the job.

If you sent a thank-you note right after the interview, the employer will remember the note when you call back. If you want the job, say so when you call the employer. If the employer has not made a decision yet, call back again in another few days or so.

If you interviewed before there was a job opening, call back from time to time to let the employer know you are still interested. The idea is to keep in touch and to make sure an employer doesn't forget you.

 checkpoint

Answer the questions that follow to review what you have learned in this chapter.

1. What are some ways you can improve how you talk about yourself?

   _____

   _____

   _____

   _____

   _____

2. How can you find information about organizations that have jobs you might want?

   _____

   _____

   _____

   _____

3. What is the value of a thank-you note after an interview?

_____

_____

_____

_____

_____

challenge: Document Your Interview

Write a newspaper article about your first interview (you will have to imagine it). Use the information you have learned in this book for your article. Write about the interview from beginning to end. Include getting ready, the interview itself, and the follow up. To get started, read the sample article below.

> Kurt Wannaget, age 21, got up on Wednesday morning, took a shower, and ate his Wheaties (Breakfast of Champions). He dressed for his interview in dark blue slacks, black shoes (recently shined), and a white shirt. Carrying a notebook containing informa- tion he might need for his application, Wannaget made sure he got to the bus stop early for the trip downtown. He arrived at Company WSB several minutes early and reported to the receptionist.

Now, continue this exercise by writing about your own interview below. Use your own paper if you run out of space.

_____

_____

_____

_____

_____

_____

chapter 20

Get Ready for the Interview and Your New Job

THE GOALS OF THIS CHAPTER ARE

- To find out how ready you are for your first interview
- To use role-playing to practice for your interviews
- To help you survive on a new job and get ahead

ARE YOU READY?

You have learned most of the basics you need to do well in your interviews. This chapter provides interview checklists, practice techniques, and some pointers to help you do well in your interviews. In addition, this chapter provides some helpful information on how to improve your chances of success at a new job.

The following Readiness Checklist will help you get organized before the interview and help prepare you to make a good impression during an interview.

FOCUS

The more confident you feel, the better you will do in your interviews.

Readiness Checklist

Imagine that you have an interview later today. Get ready by showering, getting dressed, gathering any information you need to take with you, and so on. Then use the checklist that follows to see what you thought to do and what you overlooked.

Did you remember to...

❑ Plan your transportation to the interview?

❑ Find out what kind of pay is typical for this job?

❑ Eat a good meal?

❑ Keep from drinking too much caffeine (to keep from being jittery)?

❑ Find out what you could about the organization?

❑ Arrange child care if necessary?

❑ Gather information you might need to fill out an application? (This includes references' names and telephone numbers; former employers' names and addresses; school addresses and dates of completion; and so on.)

Are your...

❑ Clothes clean, pressed, and attractive?

❑ Shoes shined?

❑ Fingernails clean?

❑ Makeup, jewelry, and cologne understated?

Do you feel...

❑ Confident and relaxed (as much as possible)?

❑ Alert and focused?

❑ Ready to answer questions (using the Three-Step Process)?

❑ Sure of what you can do to make a good impression? (Remember the three clues that an employer looks for during an interview.)

Go over this checklist again when you are getting ready for your real interviews.

checkpoint

Answer these questions. They will help you review what you learned in Part 4 of this book.

1. Go back to the start of each chapter in Part 4. Review the goals of each chapter. Decide for yourself whether you have reached the stated goals. What can you do to make sure you reach all the goals?

_____

_____

_____

_____

_____

2. Spend the time you need to work on any area of interviewing that you do not understand or do not feel comfortable with. What can you do to improve?

_____

_____

_____

_____

_____

3. If you're not sure about what to wear to your interview or on the job, ask someone you know and respect to help you pick out your clothes. List the clothes and accessories you will wear.

_____

_____

_____

_____

_____

4. Are you comfortable shaking hands with someone you don't know? If not, practice until it becomes easier. What else can you do to appear confident and self-assured?

_____

_____

_____

_____

_____

challenge: Role-Play—An Interview

This next exercise is best done with someone else. If a friend, relative, or someone else is not available, then you can practice by yourself. You are going to practice for an interview by role-playing. You will pretend that you are in a real interview. The actual role-playing begins on the next page. The following information and questions will prepare you to do your best.

You will be the job applicant. You will answer questions similar to those you practiced in Chapter 18. If you do this with another person, switch roles after you practice as job seeker. This will help each of you get a feel for how the interviewer observes a job seeker.

To make this exercise more effective, use the space below to write notes about the kind of job you plan to seek. Give these notes to the person who is role-playing as your "interviewer." Include ideas about the type of organization, what your duties would be, how many hours a week you would work, and other details. If possible, come to the role-play dressed as you plan to dress for your interviews.

_____

_____

_____

_____

_____

Part I: The Beginning

An interview often starts with a few moments of light conversation. This is the "warm up" time. With your partner, spend a few minutes saying hello, shaking hands, settling into your seats, and remarking on the weather (or whatever).

It is often helpful to make a positive comment on the organization or on something you see in the interviewer's office.

Part II: The Middle

You and the interviewer have become acquainted. Now it's time for the serious business of the interview to take place. Remember the Three-Step Process when you answer questions:

1. Understand what is really being asked.

2. Present the facts to make yourself look good.

3. Give examples to support your skills.

The following questions ask for the same kind of information as those in Chapter 18. They are not exactly the same questions, because every interviewer is different. If you have trouble answering these questions, you can refer back to Chapter 18. Make a note of the questions you found hard to answer. Practice these questions until you feel that you can handle them. Try to use the Three-Step Process to answer each one. Write your answers here.

1. Tell me about your abilities to do this job.

_____

_____

_____

_____

_____

2. Tell me about your background.

_____

_____

_____

_____

_____

3. Why are you applying for this job?

_____

_____

_____

_____

_____

4. How do I know you can do the job?

_____

_____

_____

_____

_____

_____

5. What are your best skills?

_____

_____

_____

_____

_____

6. What are your weaknesses for this job?

_____

_____

_____

_____

_____

7. What benefits do you need to be happy with a job? (_Hint:_ This could mean salary, insurance benefits, vacation, and so on.)

_____

_____

_____

_____

8. Have you ever been fired or had problems in past jobs?

_____

_____

_____

_____

9. What can you offer this organization?

_____

_____

_____

_____

10. What is your ideal job?

_____

_____

_____

_____

_____

11. Do you like a lot of responsibility?

_____

_____

_____

_____

_____

12. What are your strengths for this job?

_____

_____

_____

_____

_____

13. Why should I hire you? (This is the most important question of all!)

_____

_____

_____

_____

_____

_____

The "interviewer" can add more questions. You can ask the interviewer questions about the job. The more "real" you can make this practice interview, the more prepared you will be for your actual interviews.

Part III: The End

The interview is coming to an end. The interviewer will probably thank you for coming in.

Remember to do the following:

- Thank the interviewer for taking the time to meet with you.
- Ask for the job (if you want it).
- Ask when a good time would be to call back.

If you do want the job, you can get this across by saying something like, "I know I could do a good job for you, and I'd really like the chance to show you that."

Part IV: Follow Up

Write a brief thank-you note to your interviewer. (Make sure you have found out how to spell his or her name. When you do this after a real interview, call the receptionist or someone at the company if you're not sure how to spell the name. Or ask for the interviewer's business card at the interview.) Write your thank-you note here:

_____

_____

_____

_____

_____

_____

Imagine that it is a few days after the interview you role-played. Make a telephone call to your interviewer. Tell the interviewer why you want the job and why you think you could do it well. Write what you could say to the employer here:

_____

_____

_____

_____

_____

_____

_____

_____

_____

SURVIVING ON A NEW JOB

As you begin a new job, you will probably feel a bit of fear. Often, you don't know what to expect. Will you get along with the other people who work there? Are you dressed appropriately? Will you be able to handle the new job responsibilities?

There are things you can do to increase your chances of success on a new job. If you want to do well, you may need to change the way you act and some of your attitudes.

Why People Get Fired

Surveys of employers indicate the major reasons why a person does not do well on the job. Look at the following list of reasons why people have been fired.

- Unable to get along with other workers
- Was dishonest (lied or stole things)
- Poor dress or grooming
- Unreliable, too many days absent or late
- Used work time for personal business
- Couldn't do the work
- Worked too slowly, made too many mistakes
- Would not follow orders, did not get along with supervisor
- Abused alcohol or drugs
- Misrepresented their skills or experience
- Too many accidents, did not follow safety rules

Getting Off to a Good Start

Following the basic tips presented here can help you get off to a good start at a new job.

- _Learn all you can from the job you have,_ and do it as well as you are able. Always look for ways to put your skills to better use.

- *Be on time and don't miss work.* A minor illness, like a cold, is not a good reason for missing work. Nor are most personal problems such as child care or getting your car fixed.

- *Be careful about your grooming.* It is important that your clothes fit well, are clean, and look good. Notice how others dress in jobs similar to yours. Dress at least as well, but cleaner.

- *Find a "buddy" to help you.* New employees are often assigned to a co-worker to teach them the basics of the job. If necessary, find your own and go out of your way to be nice to this person.

- *Read personnel and procedure manuals.* Most larger organizations have manuals that give the office rules and instructions for doing various parts of the job. Ask your supervisor to explain any special procedures or rules to you.

- *Stay away from problem employees.* There are always some negative people in any workplace. Be friendly, but do not socialize with people like this any more than necessary.

- *Keep personal problems at home.* Do not spend time on personal concerns if you can avoid it. Although some socializing on the job is common, you can easily overdo it. Limit your personal activities and discussions to breaks, lunch times, or hours outside of work as much as possible.

- *Work fast, but carefully.* It is important to work at a steady and quick pace. Find a pace that you can keep up all day without making errors. You will need to make good use of breaks and lunch periods for rest.

Extra Things You Can Do to Get Ahead

If you want to be promoted or have more control over what you do on your job, there are additional things you can do to get ahead. Doing these things can help you get promotions and performance increases. Of course, your work will have to be good as well. There are no guarantees of success, but these tips will help.

- *Dress and groom for a promotion.* If you want to get ahead in an organization, dress and groom as if you work at the level you hope to reach next. This is not always possible, but at the very least, be clean and well-groomed.

- *Be early and stay late.* Get to work early and plan your day. At the end of the day, leave at least a few minutes after quitting time. Let the boss know that you are willing to stay late to meet an important deadline.

- *Be enthusiastic and ask for more responsibility.* Go out of your way to find ways to enjoy your job. Be willing to take on more responsibility. Let the boss know you want to move up.

- *Ask for training and learn on your own time.* Take any training that is available from your employer or ask for help in finding the best training source. Consider taking evening classes to help you advance on the job.

- *Take on difficult projects with measurable results.* You won't get much positive attention unless you do more than is expected of you. Look for projects you think you can do well, and would benefit the organization. Keep records of what you do.

- *Don't just quit.* Sometimes a job doesn't work out. Ask for a job change within the organization before you give up. Or be more assertive in asking your boss for more responsibility or different assignments.

CONCLUSION: STAY CONFIDENT

Congratulations! By completing Part 4, you have become a better job seeker. You are more likely to get the job you want than someone who is less skillful in interviews.

Being well prepared for job interviews can give you an edge over people who are just as qualified. If those people have not practiced interview skills, you can make a better impression.

You may go to many interviews before you find the job that's right. You can learn from each one of those interviews. Meanwhile, stay confident, and do the best you can.

You also have learned ways to survive on a new job and get ahead in the organization. Good luck in your job search, at your new job, and in your life!

index

A

accomplishments, 56, 145–149
action words (interviews), 132–134
activities and skills, 17–18, 37
adaptive skills, 18, 21, 23–26, 31–33, 46
adult education, 51
age discrimination, 134, 139
agencies, employment, 64–65
agriculture and natural resources, 47
alcohol and drug abuse, 239
ambition, 24
appearance and grooming, 122, 196, 199, 231–232, 239–240
application forms
    action words, 132–134
    appearance and grooming, 122
    availability, 177
    awards and certificates, 150–153, 178
    completing, 123
    convictions and felonies, 179
    creativity, 170
    education and training, 121, 124, 127, 150–153, 173, 179, 185
    first impressions, 118, 122–128, 169, 172, 174, 186
    honesty, 135, 145–149, 168
    information inventory, 135–142, 165–166
    job objectives, 174
    job search methods, 167
    military service, 124, 127, 152, 154–156, 181
    neatness, 169
    personal information, 120, 124, 127, 136–143, 173, 177, 183
    personal references, 162–164
    positive attitude, 169
    proofreading, 129
    qualifications, 185
    recommendations, 145–149
    references, 125, 128, 157–165, 168–169, 181
    screening process, 117–119, 122, 130
    skills, 185
    system-prompted, 129–131
    work experience, 121, 173, 177–180, 184
apprenticeships, 50–51
architecture and construction, 47
armed forces. See military service

artistic skills, 30
arts and communication, 47
assertiveness, 24
assessments
    adaptive skills, 21, 23–26
    careers, 73–75
    job-related skills, 21
    leisure skills, 15
    life experiences, 34
    life skills, 3–4
    school skills, 15
    self, 201
    skills, 14–18, 20, 35–42
    strengths and weaknesses, 209–210
    transferable skills, 21, 26–31
    volunteer experience, 38
    work skills, 15
attitude
    negative, 5–7, 52–53, 222
    positive, 18, 52–53, 77, 169, 203, 223, 230–231, 241
availability (work schedules), 137, 177
available positions, 189–191
awards and certificates, 77, 150–153, 178
awareness of skills, 21

B–C

benefits, 74, 89, 236
blaming others, 4–5
Bureau of Labor Statistics, 21
business and administration, 47

Call Back Close, 224–225
career counselors, 65
CareerBuilder.com, 73
CareerOINK, 21
careers, assessments, 72–75
certificates. See awards and certificates
challenges
    adaptive skills, 32–33
    cold contacts, 104
    confidence during interviews, 228–229
    first impressions, 175
    goals and strategies, 58
    good-worker traits, 193–194
    JIST Cards, 83

networking, 70, 89, 98
the perfect job, 166
qualifications for jobs, 166
referrals, 98
responsibility, 13
self-assessments, 201
self-employment, 43–44
skills awareness, 21
telephone calls, 112
time management, 13, 43–44
Why should I hire you?, 219
checklists. *See* challenges; worksheets
child labor laws, 139
choices for life, 3–4
chronological resumes, 75
church members, 91–93
citizenship, 137
closing (interviews), 224–225
clothes. *See* appearance and grooming
clusters. *See* job areas
co-workers, 91–93, 192, 197, 240
coaches. *See* education and training
cold contacts
    employers, 104, 106–111
    job search methods, 99–100
    networking, 100
    telephone calls, 100
colleges and universities, 49, 151–152, 159–160
cologne/perfume, 196
combination resumes, 75
communication skills, 24, 28–29, 217
community and junior colleges, 94
companies
    job markets, 62
    research, 223–224, 227
    Web sites, 223
compensation, worker's, 141
computer skills, 40–41
confidence during interviews, 220–223, 230–231
contact information, 79–81, 93, 136–137
contacts. *See* cold contacts; networking; warm
  contacts
continuing education, 51
control skills, 4, 7, 12
convictions and felonies, 140, 143, 179
country of origin, 134, 137
creative skills, 30
creativity on application forms, 170
criminal records. *See* convictions and felonies

D

data, working with, 28
deadlines, meeting, 24, 197
dependability, 24
disabilities, people with, 134, 140–141, 182
discrimination, 134, 139–141
dishonesty. *See* honesty

documentation for portfolios, 78
Dowjones.com, 73
dress. *See* appearance and grooming
driver's licenses, 141
dropping in on employers, 112
drug and alcohol abuse, 239

E

e-mails, 225–226
education and training, 35–37, 47, 241
    application forms, 121, 124, 127, 150–153, 173,
      179, 185
    apprenticeships, 50
    colleges and universities, 49
    community college, 49
    continuing education, 51–52
    high school, 36–37, 49
    Internet, 52, 204–205
    junior high school/middle school, 35–36
    libraries, 52
    location, 49–50
    military service, 50–51
    on-the-job training, 50
    references, 159–162
    resources, 51–52
    resumes, 76
    self-directed, 51
    time management, 49
    vocational and technical schools, 49
elementary school, 150
employers, 91–93. *See also* work experience
    adaptive skills, 25
    cold contacts, 99–102, 104, 160–109
    first impressions, 195–197
    help wanted advertisements, 67–68
    interviews, 200
    job markets, 68–69
    networking, 49, 94
    on-the-job training, 50
    recommendations, 88
    skills and qualifications, 20
    telephone calls, 106–111
    walk-in appointments, 112
    warm contacts, 85
    yellow pages, 100–103
employment. *See* employers; work experience
employment agencies, 64–67, 70
enthusiasm, 240
equipment on the job, 145–146
Exploring Careers, 72
extracurricular activities, 36–37

F

failure and risk, 57
family/relatives, 91–93
fees (employment agencies), 65, 70

felonies and convictions, 140, 143, 179

finance and insurance, 47

financial aid, 49

fired from jobs, 236, 239

first impressions

    appearance and grooming, 196

    application forms, 118, 122–128, 169, 172,
      174–175, 186

    employers, 195–197

    interviews, 190–192

    JIST Cards, 80–81

555–1212.com, 73

flexibility, 24

follow-up

    interviews, 225–226, 238

    telephone calls, 227

    thank-you notes, 228

following instructions, 18, 24

four-year colleges and universities, 94

friends (networking), 90–91

full-time jobs, 138

G

GED (General Equivalency Diploma), 151

goals, 53–58, 232

good attendance, 24

good-worker traits, 191–194

government and public administration, 47, 62

government employment agencies, 65–67

grammar, 77, 129

guidance counselors, 91–93

H

handshaking, 196, 233–234

hard-working, 24, 192

health issues, 141

health science, 47

help wanted advertisements, 64, 66–69

hidden job markets, 67–70, 85, 95

high school, 36–37, 49, 150–151, 161

hobbies, 15–17, 40–41, 215

honesty (application forms), 18, 24, 77, 135, 145,
    168, 192, 239

Hoover's Online, 73

hospitality, tourism, and recreation, 47

human services, 47

humor, sense of, 24

hygiene, personal, 196

I

illegal questions, 134–135, 139

improvement of skills, 41–42

information inventory

    application forms, 135–142

education and training, 150–152

    personal information, 143

information technology, 47

InfoUSA.com, 73

instructions, following, 18, 24

interest areas. *See* job areas

Internet. *See also* Web sites

    education and training, 52

    leads, 103

    research, 73

    system-prompted application forms, 129–131

interviews, 193. *See also* questions

    appearance and grooming, 199, 231–232

    closing, 224–225

    confidence, 220–223, 230–231

    employers, 107, 200

    first impressions, 190–192, 195–197

    follow up, 225–226, 238

    introductions, 234

    listening skills, 204

    modesty, 220

    networking, 94

    positive attitude, 203, 230–231

    preparation, 228, 231–232

    punctuality, 197

    questions, 17, 22, 46, 202–204, 217, 223–224,
      234–237

    role-playing, 233–238

    selling yourself, 197–199

    skills, 17–18, 200

    speaking, 221–223, 227

    strengths and weaknesses, 235–237

    telephone calls, 227

    thank-you notes, 225–226, 228

    Three-Step Process, 203–215, 218

    work experience, 222

introductions (interviews), 234

inventory information

    application forms, 165–166

    education and training, 36

    extracurricular activities, 36–37

    military experience, 47, 154–156

    personal information, 136–143

    professional organizations, 37

    skills, 35–42, 45

    work experience, 38, 42–43, 144–149

J–K

JIST Cards, 79

    contact information, 80–81

    first impressions, 80–81

    job objectives, 80–81

    job search methods, 82–83

    networking, 82

    proofreading, 80

    skills, 80–81

    Web site, 73

job areas, 72–73
- agriculture and natural resources, 47
- architecture and construction, 47
- arts and communications, 47
- business and administration, 47
- career assessments, 75
- education and training, 47
- finance and insurance, 47
- government and public administration, 47
- health science, 47
- hospitality, tourism, and recreation, 47
- human services, 47
- information technology, 47
- law and public safety, 47
- manufacturing, 47
- research, 48, 57
- resources, 57
- retail and wholesale sales and service, 47
- scientific research, engineering, and mathematics, 47
- skills statements, 47–48
- transportation, distribution, and logistics, 48

job leads
- Internet, 103
- networking, 85, 95, 170–172
- referrals, 97–98
- yellow pages, 100–102, 104

job markets, 61, 63
- employers, 67–69
- government jobs, 62
- hidden, 67–70
- large companies, 62
- medium-sized companies, 62
- networking, 68, 95
- small companies, 62–63
- warm contacts, 85

job objectives, 71–72, 192–193
- application forms, 174
- career assessments, 74
- JIST Cards, 79–81
- job areas, 72–73
- qualification, 166
- resumes, 76

job performance, 118, 130, 192, 195, 239

job possibilities worksheet, 72

job search methods, 63
- application forms, 167
- cold contacts, 99
- employment agencies, 64–65
- help wanted advertisements, 64, 66, 69
- JIST Cards, 82–83
- job markets, 68
- large companies, 69
- networking, 93
- portfolios, 78
- referrals, 97–98

- resumes, 78
- small companies, 69
- telephone calls, 106–113
- traditional, 66
- warm contacts, 84–87
- workshops, 65

jobs
- offers, necessary benefits, 236
- openings, 138, 189–191
- related skills, 19, 21, 46
- temporary, 66
- terminations, 236, 239
- titles, 106

junior high school/middle school, 35–36, 150

L

labor laws, 139

large companies, 62, 69

law and public safety, 47

leadership skills, 24, 29–30

leads
- Internet, 103
- jobs, 65
- networking, 85, 170–172
- referrals, 97–98
- yellow pages, 100–102, 104

leisure skills, 15–17, 40–41, 215

libraries, research, 52, 72–73

life assessments, 3–4

life choices, 12

life experiences, 35–42

listening skills, 204

M

makeup, 196

management
- money, 18, 43
- people, 18
- time, 7–13, 20, 43, 49, 55–56

manufacturing, 47

marital status, 139, 143

maturity, 24

medium-sized companies, 62

meeting deadlines, 24, 197

middle school/junior high school, 35–36, 150

military service, 37, 152
- application forms, 124, 127, 154–156, 181
- education and training, 50–51
- Web sites, 51

mistakes, 4–5

modesty (interviews), 220

money management, 18, 43

Monster.com, 73

motivation, 24

N

national origin, 134, 137
neatness on application forms, 169
negative attitude, 5–7, 52–53, 222
negotiations, salary, 216
neighbors, 91–93
networking
    benefits, 89
    challenges, 70, 98
    church members, 91–93
    co-workers, 91–93
    cold contacts, 99–100
    contact lists, 93
    employers, 48, 91–94
    family/relatives, 91–93
    friends, 90–91
    goal planning, 54
    guidance counselors, 91–93
    hidden job markets, 68
    interviews, 94
    JIST Cards, 79, 82
    job leads, 85, 95, 170–172
    neighbors, 91–93
    parents, 91–93
    professional organizations, 91–93
    recommendations, 88
    referrals, 96–98
    warm contacts, 84–88
New Guide for Occupational Exploration, 72

O–P

objectives (jobs), 71–72, 174, 192–193
Occupational Outlook Handbook, 72
on-the-job training, 50
openings (jobs), 189–191
organizational skills, 27
overtime work, 138

parents, 91–93
part-time jobs, 138
patience, 24
people management, 18, 28–29
the "perfect job", 166, 213
performance on the job, 118, 130, 192, 195, 239
perfume/cologne, 196
persistence, 24
personal hygiene, 196
personal information
    application forms, 120, 124, 127, 136–143, 173, 177, 183
    JIST Cards, 79
personal problems, 240
personal references, 162–164
personality. *See* adaptive skills
personnel departments, avoiding, 106–107, 111

personnel manuals, 240
phone calls. *See* telephone calls
physical limitations, 141
portfolios, documentation, 77–78
positive attitude, 18, 52–53, 77, 169, 203, 223, 230–231, 240–241
posture, 197
preparation for interviews, 228, 231–232
presentations during interviews, 202
private employment agencies, 65–67, 70
problem-solving skills, 18
procedure manuals, 240
professional organizations, 37, 91–93
progress tracking, 56–57
project management, 241
promotions, 145–159, 240–241
proofreading resumes and application forms, 77, 80, 129
punctuality, 24, 192, 240

Q

qualifications and employers, 20, 166, 185
quality of life, 3–4
questions. *See also* interviews
    Can you tell me a little about yourself?, 206
    How well do you handle responsibility?, 214
    How would you help make our organization better?, 212
    illegal, 134–135, 139
    interviews, 17, 22, 46, 202–204, 217, 223–224, 234–237
    positive attitude, 203
    referrals, 97–98
    salary, 216
    Three-Step Process, 203–215, 218
    What are your strongest skills for this job?, 209–210
    What areas are you weak in?, 210
    What do you like to do in your spare time?, 215
    What sorts of problems have you had in previous jobs?, 211
    What would your perfect job be?, 213
    Why do you want this job?, 207
    Why should I hire you?, 208, 219

R

race discrimination, 134
recognition. *See* awards and certificates
recommendations
    application forms, 145–149
    employers, 88
references
    application forms, 125, 128, 157–165, 181, 185
    education and training, 159–162

high schools, 161
    personal, 162–164
    work experience, 157–159
referrals
    challenges, 98
    networking, 96–98
    questions, 97–98
relatives/family, 91–93
reliability, 118, 130, 195, 197, 239
religious discrimination, 134
requirements, salary, 138–139
researching companies, 48, 57, 72–73, 223–224, 227
resources for education and training, 51–52, 57
responsibility, 4–7, 12–13, 214, 237, 240
resumes. *See also* application forms
    action words, 77
    chronological resumes, 75
    combination resumes, 75
    education and training, 76
    grammar, 77
    honesty, 77
    job objectives, 76
    job search methods, 78
    proofreading, 77
    skills resumes, 75–76
    spelling, 77
    work experience, 76
    writing, 77
retail and wholesale sales and service, 47
risk and failure, 57
role-playing (interviews), 233–238

S

salary, 74, 138–139, 216
schedules, work, 137
scholarships, 49
school skills, 15–16
schools. *See* education and training
scientific research, engineering, and mathematics, 47
screening process (application forms), 117–119, 122, 130
searches. *See* job search methods
self-assessments, 201
self-confidence, 223, 227
self-directed training, 51
self-employment, 43–44
self-management skills. *See* adaptive skills
selling yourself, 197–199
sense of humor, 24
shaking hands, 196, 233–234
sincerity, 24
skills
    adaptive skills, 18, 21, 23–26, 31–33, 46
    application forms, 185
    artistic, 30
    assessments, 3–4, 14–18, 20

    awareness, 21
    choices, 12
    communication, 28–29, 217
    computers, 40–41
    control, 7, 12
    education and training, 35–37
    good-worker traits, 191–194
    improvements, 41–42
    interviews, 17–18, 200
    inventory, 35–42, 45
    JIST Cards, 79–81
    job areas, 48
    job-related skills, 19, 46
    leadership, 29–30
    leisure, 15–17
    life choices, 3–4
    listening, 204
    money management, 18
    organizational, 27
    people management, 18, 28–29
    problem-solving, 18
    responsibility, 214
    resumes, 75–76
    school, 15–16
    skills statements, 46
    Skills Triangle, 18–21
    strengths and weaknesses, 209–210
    taking responsibility, 4–7, 12
    time management, 7–11, 20
    transferable skills, 18, 21, 26–32, 46
    unpaid work, 16
    volunteer experience, 38
    words and ideas, 28–29
    work experience, 38, 42–43, 145–149
    working with data, 28
    working with things, 27–28
small companies, 62–63, 69
SMART goals, 53–56
Social Security numbers, 137
speaking with confidence, 221–223, 227
spell-checking, 77, 129
strategies, 58
strengths and weaknesses, 209–210, 235–237
supervisors, cold contacts, 106
system-prompted application forms, 129–131

T

taking responsibility, 5–7
teachers. *See* education and training
technical school, 151–152, 159–160
telephone calls, 227, 238
    challenges, 112
    cold contacts, 100
    employers, 106–111
    job search methods, 106–113
temporary jobs, 66
terminations, 236, 239

thank-you notes, 225–226, 228, 238
Three-Step Process, 203–215, 218
time management, 7–13, 20, 43, 49, 55–56
tools/equipment on the job, 145–146
Top 300 Careers, 72
tracking progress, 56–57
trade school, 151–152, 159–160
training. *See* education and training
traits, good-worker, 191–194
transferable skills, 18, 21, 26–32, 46
transportation, distribution, and logistics, 48, 138
trustworthiness, 118, 130

U–V

unemployment, 65
universities and colleges, 49, 151–152, 159–160
unpaid work, 16

Vault.com, 73
vocational technical colleges, 49
volunteer experience, 38

W

walk-in appointments, 112
warm contacts (networking), 84–88
weaknesses and strengths, 235–237
Web sites. *See also* Internet
    America's Career InfoNet, 73
    Bureau of Labor Statistics, 21
    CareerBuilder.com, 73
    CareerOINK, 21
    companies, 223
    dowjones.com, 73
    Hoover's Online, 73
    InfoUSA.com, 73
    JIST, 73
    military service, 51
    Monster.com, 73
    research, 48
    Social Security Administration, 137
    Vault.com, 73
    yellow pages, 103

words and ideas, 29
work experience, 204–205, 211. *See also* employers
    application forms, 121, 144–149, 173, 177–178, 180, 184
    education and training, 179
    interviews, 222
    JIST Cards, 79
    promotions, 145–149
    references, 157–159
    schedules, 137
    skills, 15–16, 38, 42–43, 145–149
    unpaid, 16
worker's compensation, 141
working conditions, 74
working with data, 28
working with things, 27–28
worksheets
    action words, 132–134
    adaptive skills, 23–26
    application forms, 168
    education and training, 150–152
    goal planning, 53–56
    interview preparation, 231
    job objectives, 192–193
    job possibilities, 72
    military service, 154–156
    personal information, 136–143
    reference, 157–164
    skills inventory, 35–42
    SMART goals, 53–56
    speaking with confidence, 221–223
    time management, 8–10
    transferable skills, 26–31
    work experience, 144–149
    yellow pages, 101–102
workshops, 65
writing resumes, 77

X–Z

yellow pages, 100–103
Young Person's Occupational Outlook Handbook, 72